Lets Eat!

Italian

For my Mother Mary,
my Grandparents who brought with them from Italy
a culture rich in tradition.

Forward

Traveling, Art, Music and Good Food are high on my list of pleasures. Italian cooking is all of that. Cooking genuine Italian food is not difficult, but it is at times labor intensive. I have always believed that the effort is well worth it.

The cooking you find in restaurants that call themselves Italian, with a few exceptions, is part-Italian, part- American and part invented. They believe if they put oregano and tomato sauce on it becomes Italian, they make dishes that no Italian would recognize as part of his or her heritage.

I have decided there is another way to get good Italian food on the table. Cook it yourself. This book includes a lot of my favorite dishes, which are made with fresh ingredients readily found and available. Do not substitute with inferior ingredients! If you do not have the ingredient, do not make it. Instead make something else be creative. Remember Italians always eat what is in season. Enjoy the process, in the shopping, the preparation, the cooking and of course the eating. It is very rewarding.

I always wondered why the food in Italy varies from region to region. My belief is each region had different ingredients. So, recipes vary.

This book is a collection of recipes from my trips to Italy and many family recipes. I have tried to keep the recipes as pure and as simple as possible. This book gave me a great opportunity to continue my exploration as I am always learning .

Italian cooking is an art and it should be treated as art. Like a painting, you can change it, rearrange it, but know when to stop. Less is always more. "The most important ingredient in Italian Cooking is the one you leave out" . - Marcella Hassan

Italians always talk about food because they always treat it as a work of art which can invite rich discussion. I never hear anybody having a conversation about a Big Mac and fries. What is there to say? I rest my case.

Most all the courses are interchangeable. Remember there is no main course but a series of plates e.g. Il Primo, Il Secondo and Contorni either maybe considered as a main course but each course is served separately.

Perhaps I can persuade you to give it a try. Next time you prepare a meal, listen to the music, travel to Italy, create your own masterpiece and ...

Let's Eat! Italian

ODE TO AN OLD WOODEN SPOON

From whence it came, just can't be said,
perhaps from one generation onto next.
Long and scooped out at one end,
its slender handle extended to the other.
Its wood, amply seasoned by its years of use,
was well infused, by essence of its handlers too.

There was Mom, who with this very spoon,
stirred and scraped, tossed and mixed,
and heaped our plates as she lovingly
served the food that nourished us.

It stirred the bubbling, thick pea soup,
as it spouted and puffed in its cook pot;
Or, the dried white beans, or lentils,
as they melted into softened tenderness.
It helped build the hearty minestrone,
an amalgam of sweet flavored vegetables.
It tugged at the frying onions, peppers,
and potatoes, sticking in their pan.

It turned the meatballs or sausages,
simmering in the Sunday pasta sauce.
It helped sauté the mushroom slices,
or escarole in the hot oil and garlic mix.

It churned the slow cooking stews of meat,
and chunky vegetables in savory sauce.
It untangled the cooking pasta
in the boiling, roiling water of the pot.
Endlessly, it stirred the polenta as it huffed
and puffed, slowly thickening in its bronze pot.
There was mixing of cake batter and icing,
and the joy of children licking the spoon.

Aside from food, the spoon found other uses too.
Mom wagged it menacingly at her misbehaving
brood, an idle threat that made its point.
A tot, with paper soldier hat, shouldered
and pointed it as his make-believe weapon.
The banging of pots to usher in the New Year.
Now, as we grip its wooden handle, held by those
that came before, we sense the essence of their memories
that caress our very souls.

Albert Balossi

Contents

Antipasti

Pasta

Prima Piatti

Pasta/Risotto/Zuppa

Secondo Piatti

Carne/Pesce/Polenta

Contorni

Vedura

Insalata/Fritatta

Pane

Bread/ Pizza/ Focaccia

Savory Pies

Dolce

Bibita

Antipasti

Bruschetta con Pomodoro
Parmesan Toast
Tonno Sotto'Olio
Bruschetta with Anchovies
Crostini with Chicken Livers
Tuna Spread with Capers
Prosciutto wrapped Asparagus
Capri Salad
Grilled Vegetables
Caponata
Stuffed Mushrooms
Cipollini Agrodolce
Marinated Zucchini
Giardiniera / Pickled Vegetables
Pickled Eggplant
Fried Olives
Sicilian-Style Olives
Mozzarella in Carrozza
Mozzarella with Herbs
Chickpea Fritters
Fried Zucchini Flowers
Bread Salad
Frito Misto

Antipasto means "before the meal" and is the traditional first course of a formal Italian meal. Antipasto is served at the table and signifies the beginning of the Italian meal. Most table settings will feature a central antipasto plate, and small plates for each diner to enjoy this warm-up to the other courses.

Antipasto can consist of many things. The most traditional offerings are cured meats, marinated vegetables, olives, peperoni (not to be confused with the meat), which are marinated small peppers, and various cheeses, perhaps provolone, or fresh mozzarella. Other additions may be anchovies, or bruschetta, toasted bread, upon which one may stack the meats or cheeses. The antipasto is usually topped off with some extra virgin olive oil.

Antipasti Misti Salumi

Salumi is the Italian word for cold cuts, which include salami in English, prosciutto, pancetta, cured lard, sausages, mortadella, Capocollo, Sopressada, and Speck and all sorts of other treats.

Antipasti Misti

Contains an assortment of cooked or marinated vegetables, beans, tuna, cheese, anchovies and olives.

Seafood Antipasti

Shrimp, Calamare, Octopus, Tuna, Anchovies, Clams and Muscles

Pinzimonio

This is more of a suggestion than a recipe; pinzimonio can be a tasty antipasto. It's wonderful and refreshing.
Vegetables Olive Oil Salt and Pepper
Prepare a big bowl of fresh tasty vegetables, cut into strips or pieces e.g. (peppers, cauliflower, artichokes, celery, carrots, etc.).
Set cruets of olive oil and vinegar on the table, along with salt & pepper.

Bruschetta

Bruschetta is an antipasti or part of an antipasto. It consists of toasted bread rubbed with garlic and topped with extra-virgin olive oil, salt, and pepper. Variations may include toppings of roasted red peppers, tomato, vegetables, beans, cured meat, or cheese; a popular recipe in Italy is fresh basil, fresh tomato, mozzarella and thinly sliced prosciutto crudo.

Bruschetta con Pomodoro
Bruschetta with Tomatoes

8 (1/2-inch thick) slices Italian country bread
1/4 cup extra-virgin olive oil
6 small ripe but firm tomatoes, halved, and diced
1 clove garlic, minced
8 fresh basil leaves, torn or chopped
Red pepper flakes to taste
1/4 teaspoon coarse salt

In a bowl, combine the olive oil, tomatoes, minced garlic, red pepper, and salt. Set aside for at least 60 minutes to marinate.
Preheat an outdoor grill or grill pan to medium heat.
Grill the bread until it is browned on both sides, about 2 minutes per side. While still warm, rub each side with the cut garlic. Divide the tomato mixture on top of each bread slice. Arrange on a platter and serve.
The addition of mozzarella cheese into small cubes gives added taste and texture.

Bruschetta con Parmigiano
Parmesan Toasts

8 1/4-inch-thick slices Italian bread
1 medium garlic clove, halved
Extra-virgin olive oil, 1/2 cup finely grated Parmesan cheese
Preheat oven to 400F. Arrange bread on baking sheet. Rub bread with garlic; drizzle with oil. Sprinkle cheese over. Sprinkle with salt. Bake until edges are lightly browned, about 12 minutes.

My mother would quickly dip one side in milk, and then add the cheese drizzle with oil. then bake either way. It's good.

Tonno Sott'olio

Tuna in olive oil

2 cloves garlic
1 bay leaf
A couple black peppercorns
Fresh tuna, cut into large chunks
extra-virgin olive oil

Purchase some fresh tuna cut in large chunks and put it in a small sauce pan (small pot helps reduce the amount of oil you need). Combine the garlic, bay leaf and spices. Cover in extra virgin olive oil and cook (simmer slowly) for about 10 to 15 minutes until tuna is cooked all the way through. Make sure the fish does not fry, keep heat very low just enough to poach. Drain the tuna and place in a jar (salt if you like).
Cover with olive oil and seal. Refrigerate a day or two.

A real treat. Tuna in olive oil. Easy to do and better than any canned tuna.

Bruschetta con Acciuga
Bruschetta with Anchovies

Slices of Italian country style bread
8 Anchovy fillets (usually a small can)
1 Garlic clove
Chopped parsley or a pinch of good oregano
Olive Oil
Red pepper flakes

In a small pan sauté the garlic clove in the olive oil and remove when golden, not brown. Add the minced anchovies, red pepper flakes and allow infusing for 1 to 2 minutes.
Place the bread on the grill and toast. Drizzle the infused anchovy and oil over the bruschetta, garnish with parsley.

Crostini di Fegatini di Polio
Chicken Liver Crostini

1 small onion
3 tbsp olive oil
1/2 lb. chicken livers
1/4 cup Dry Marsala or Vin Santo wine
Salt and Pepper
4 anchovy fillets
1 Tablespoon capers, rinsed
3/4 stick unsalted butter
Tuscan sliced bread

Chop the onions finely, sauté gently in the olive oil.

Cut the chicken livers into small pieces, add to the onions, and cook for a few minutes.

Pour in the Marsala or Vin Santo and simmer until the liquid has almost evaporated. Season the chicken livers with salt and pepper, and sauté for another 5 min. Let cool slightly, then place in a food processor with the anchovy fillets, the capers, and the butter, and blend to a very fine purée.

Toast the slices of bread in the oven and spread thickly with paste. Serve warm or cold.

A Tuscan meal would not be complete without chicken liver crostini, Thin slices of toasted bread spread with a tasty chicken liver pate that even makes converts out of liver haters.

Tonno Sott'olio Mantecato

Tuna Spread with Capers

Two 6 1/2-ounce cans Italian-style tuna packed in olive oil
1 to 2 tablespoons capers rinsed
8 tablespoons unsalted butter: Soften to room temperature

Drain the tuna of all the oil in which it was packed. Put the tuna, capers, and butter in a food Processor. Whip to creamy consistency.
The spread can be served in a bowl or spread on crostini. If made ahead and refrigerated, it should be taken out of the refrigerator at least 45 minutes ahead of time so that it can soften to its original creamy consistency.
I like to garnish each with finely chopped parsley or a few capers or both.

Asparagi con Prosciutto

Prosciutto Wrapped Asparagus

Asparagus,
trimmed and peeled if needed
Prosciutto thinly sliced
Coarsely ground black pepper

Boil water over high heat. Add asparagus; cook 3 minutes to blanch Drain; rinse with cold running water, dry with paper towels. Wrap prosciutto in spiral along length of asparagus add fresh ground pepper. Arrange on platter and serve.

Insalata Caprese
Capri Salad

Tomatoes and mozzarella with olive oil and basil. It does need the freshest ingredients, Sun-ripened tomatoes and basil, good Mozzarella, from buffalo milk if possible, and extra virgin olive oil.

Ripe tomatoes, sliced, sliced 1/4 inch thick
A fresh mozzarella (buffalo milk if possible)
Fresh basil leaves, hand-shredded
3 to 4 tablespoons or to taste
Pepper and coarse salt to taste
A pinch of oregano (optional)

Slice the mozzarella into rounds and put them on plates; slice the tomatoes into and lay them over the tomatoes. Drizzle extra virgin olive oil over the mozzarella and tomato. Tear the basil leaves into pieces by hand and sprinkle on top. Season with salt and pepper and serve.

There are Campani in the region of Campania who also add a little oregano. You can omit it if you wish.

Verdure alla Griglia
Grilled Antipasto Platter

Garlic and Herb Oil
Extra virgin olive oil
Balsamic or Red wine vinegar
2 cloves garlic, chopped
4 sprigs fresh Rosemary, fresh Basil or Parsley chopped
Kosher salt and freshly ground black pepper

Vegetables
Extra-virgin olive oil, plus more as needed and for garnish
1 to 2 medium eggplant, sliced
2 to 4 medium zucchini, sliced
3 to 4 red bell peppers, halved and cored
or any other vegetable not listed
1 Red onion sliced
olives, for garnish (optional)
Fresh herbs for garnish

Heat the grill to low. Brush with olive oil. Coat the eggplant, zucchini and peppers, separately with the oil. Grill the vegetables, basting generously with the Garlic and Herb Oil, until tender and soft: about 10 minutes for the eggplant, 8 minutes for the zucchini and onion, and about 15 minutes for the peppers. Arrange them on a large platter and garnish with the olives, and herbs. Drizzle over the remaining Herbed Oil and season with salt and pepper.

Caponata

Eggplant Appetizer

1 or 2 medium Eggplant
Coarse salt
1/3 to 1/2 cup olive oil
4 large stalks of celery cut into large dice
1 large onion, coarsely chopped
1 red pepper, diced.
12 green Sicilian olives, pitted and coarsely chopped
4 anchovy fillets, rinsed and coarsely chopped (optional)
3 tablespoons capers, rinsed
2 tablespoons chopped Italian parsley or fresh basil
2 to 4 tablespoons red-wine vinegar
1 to 2 teaspoons sugar, or to taste
3 tablespoons tomato paste, or 3 plum tomatoes diced
Salt and Red pepper flakes to taste

Cut the eggplant into 1/2-inch cubes. Place the eggplant in a colander and sprinkle with the coarse salt. Let stand and drain for about 20 minutes, or until the dark juices have drained off. Pat the eggplant dry with paper towels.

In a heavy skillet, heat 1/3 cup of the oil and add the celery, pepper, garlic and onion. Sauté over low heat for about 5 minutes or until the vegetables are translucent, but not brown. Add the eggplant and sauté slowly until it begins to color. If the mixture is too dry, add the remaining oil. Add the olives, anchovies, capers, parsley, or basil, 2 tablespoons of vinegar and sugar. Dissolve the tomato paste in 3 tablespoons of water and add to the dish. Simmer gently, partially covered, for about 10 minutes, adding a little water if needed to prevent scorching. Uncover and simmer an; other 5 minutes, or until the juices evaporate. Season with salt and the red pepper. Serve at room temperature.

A Sicilian favorite and is served as part of an antipasto.

Funghi Ripieni
Stuffed Mushrooms

Large mushrooms
Garlic chopped
Butter
Olive Oil
Breadcrumbs, seasoned with parsley and cheese
Salt and pepper to taste
Chopped parsley
Water
Grated Romano cheese (or Parmesan) to taste
Extra virgin olive oil (just keep the whole bottle handy)

Preheat oven to 350 F .
Clean mushrooms thoroughly.
Cut off mushroom stems and chop fine. Sauté stems in equal amounts
of olive oil, butter, and the chopped garlic.
In a bowl mix breadcrumbs, parsley, and sautéed mushroom stems.
Add grated cheese, plus salt and pepper to taste.
Mix together with add enough water to moisten (1 to 2) tablespoons)
and fill the mushrooms then place on a baking pan.
Sprinkle with olive oil.
Bake at 350 F for 20 to 30 minutes or until mushrooms are done
Serve warm.

Every holiday there was always stuffed mushrooms on the table.

Cipollini Agrodolce
Sweet and Sour Onions

4 tablespoons extra-virgin olive oil
1 to 1/2 pounds small white cipollini onions
1/3 cup sugar
1/2 to1 cup red wine or balsamic vinegar
1 cup water
Salt and pepper

Blanch onions in boiling water to remove skins 2 to three minutes.
In a large, heavy-bottomed saucepan, combine all ingredients, cover,
and bring to a boil. Reduce to a simmer and cook, shaking the pan
occasionally so that the onions do not stick to the bottom of the pan.
The onions should be easily penetrated with a knife but should not
be falling apart.
Remove the lid and continue to cook until the liquid has evaporated,
and the onions are glossy and dark brown, taking care not to burn.
Remove from heat and serve at room temperature.

Cipollini are smaller, flat, pale onions. They can be a little difficult to find.
Specialty markets and grocery stores will have them.

Le Zucchine a Scapece
Marinated Zucchini

4 medium zucchini, trimmed and cut crosswise into 1/8 to 1/4 inches
thick round slices
Oil for frying
Red wine or balsamic vinegar
fresh mint (optional)
2 cloves garlic, chopped or thinly sliced
Olive oil
Coarse salt and freshly ground pepper

Pour oil into a wide medium pan to a depth of 1/2" and heat over
medium-high heat until temperature reaches about 350 F.
Meanwhile, pick leaves from 4 sprigs of the mint, coarsely chop, and
set aside.
Working in batches, fry zucchini in hot oil until lightly browned and
soft, 5-6 minutes per batch be sure not to crowd. Transfer zucchini
with a slotted spoon to paper towels to drain.
Arrange the zucchini in a medium dish. Sprinkle the vinegar,
chopped mint, and garlic over zucchini and season to taste with salt
and pepper. Cover dish with plastic wrap and refrigerate overnight.
Serve zucchini at room temperature, garnished with mint leaves.

They are typical of the Cucina di Campania.
Like most marinated vegetable dishes, this one is best made a day ahead of
serving. It will keep, refrigerated, for about a week. Absolutely addictive!

Giardiniera

Pickled Vegetables

10 ounces pearl onions, peeled and soaked in cold water for an hour
10 ounces carrots, peeled and diagonally sliced or cut into sticks about 2 inches long
10 ounces celery, stalks only, cut into short lengths
A small cauliflower
1 large green pepper
1 large red pepper
1-quart white vinegar
2 quarts water
Olive oil
A couple of bay leaves
2-3 garlic cloves
1 teaspoon black peppercorns
1 tablespoon salt
1/2 teaspoon Red pepper flakes or to taste

Mix the vinegar and water with the herbs, spices, and salt. Separate the cauliflower florets. Add the vegetables to a large non-corrosive jar or pot and cover them with liquid. Let sit 3 days to a week in a cool place making sure all the vegetables are submerged in liquid. Remove them to the jars with a slotted spoon and add olive oil. Cover them tightly and let them cool. Store them in the refrigerator for a couple of weeks, and they are ready for use. Expect them to keep for a year. * (This is not a canning method and should be refrigerated for storage)

This is what most Italians think of when they hear the words Sotto Aceti or Sotto Olio, a collection of mixed pickled vegetables. The standard Italian antipasto misto would not be quite right without these; I like this method because the vegetables are always crisp.

Melanzane Marinate
Pickled Eggplant

1 to 2 Eggplants
Kosher Salt
White Vinegar
3 to 4 cloves garlic, sliced thin
1/4 to 1/2 teaspoon red pepper flakes (optional)
1 or 2 green or red bell pepper, sliced into strips
Olive Oil

Slice the eggplant thinly, and then cut the slices into thin strips.
Layer the strips in a colander and mix with some Kosher Salt. Place the
colander in the sink, put a dish on top of it, and put something heavy on
top of the dish to weigh it down, as this helps take the bitterness out of
the eggplant. After one hour, squeeze the eggplant.
In a large non-corrosive pot place the sliced garlic, the eggplant,
peppers, and garlic. Cover with a ratio of 2 cups of water to 1 cup of the
vinegar. Put something heavy on top of the dish to weigh it down. Let
soak 3 to 4 days or up to a week. Drain and squeeze. Place the eggplant
in a jar pressing down to remove any air. Leave about an inch at the top.
Pour in olive oil so that all the eggplant is submerged. Cover with a lid
and let marinate for a week in the refrigerator.

*The peppers really give this eggplant a wonderful taste. My mother always had
some pickled eggplant in the refrigerator. it is a great addition to any meal or
Antipasto.*
Mangia!

Olive Fritte
Fried Olives

3 tablespoons olive oil
2 cloves garlic, thinly sliced
1 teaspoon dried oregano or thyme
oil cured olives dry
1 teaspoon wine vinegar
Zest of lemon or orange
Salt and pepper to taste

In a medium skillet, combine olive oil, garlic and oregano and heat on low for 1 to 2 minutes. Add olives and vinegar, orange zest, and pepper and stir well to combine. Cook for 2 to 3 minutes. Serve warm with crunchy bread.

My cousin Serina in Sicily would always fry up some black oil cured olives just plain and drizzle with olive oil and a touch of red pepper flakes, serving them hot with bread as a welcoming snack or a treat.

Oliva Cunzati
Sicilian-Style Olives

"Green olives dressed with celery, onion, olive oil, vinegar and oregano."

1-pound large green Sicilian olives, crushed lightly to expose pits*
3 stalks celery hearts with leaves, medium diced
1 small red onion, medium diced or 2 to 3 cloves of garlic smashed
(I like the garlic)
2 teaspoons dried oregano
1/3 cup olive oil
1 teaspoon red wine vinegar
hot red pepper flakes
Coarse ground black pepper (optional)

Mix all ingredients including the black pepper if using, in a medium nonreactive bowl. Refrigerate, tossing occasionally, for 4 hours. Keep refrigerated but serve at room temperature.

*Green Sicilian olives are available at Italian markets and in the Italian section of many supermarkets. *Crush the olives with a meat mallet or the flat surface of a chef's knife until they split, and their pits are exposed. This will allow the flavors of the red onion, oregano, and vinegar to permeate the olives.*

This was a staple at my grandmother's table. I remember they were always on the table and there was always a jar in the refrigerator.

Mozzarella in Carrozza
Fried Mozzarella

Fresh Mozzarella sliced
1 egg, lightly beaten
Breadcrumbs (seasoned)
Flour
Oil for frying

Begin by slicing the mozzarella and pat dry and setting side: dust with flour and then dredge the slices in the beaten egg, and then in the seasoned breadcrumbs, put them on a cookie sheet lined with wax paper, and chill them in the freezer for a 1 hour.

Fry the mozzarella disks for about a minute in hot oil carefully turning once. Arrange them on a serving dish, salt them well, and serve them at once.

A side of spicy marinara sauce for dipping is great.

Mozzarella alle Erbe
Mozzarella with Herbs

Mozzarella, cut into bite-size pieces
Extra-virgin olive oil
Fresh basil chopped
Fresh parsley chopped
Oregano (optional)
Bay leaf
Salt and Red pepper flakes, to taste

Combine all ingredients in a bowl and mix well. Cover and refrigerate for several hours or overnight. Remove bay leaf and serve at room temperature.

Panella

Chickpea Fritters

1 cup chickpea flour
2 cups water
Lemon juice
Coarse salt and fresh ground pepper to taste
2 tablespoons chopped fresh parsley
Oil for frying

Combine the chickpea flour and water until smooth. Place in a saucepan over medium-low heat and bring to a low boil. Add the salt, pepper, and parsley.

Stir constantly with a wooden spoon until you obtain a soft, lump-free paste or until the mixture thickens, about 4-5 minutes or when the paste begins to pull away from the sides of the pot. Spread it out onto an oiled baking sheet before it cools. Spread an even layer that is 1/4 to1/2-inch thick rectangle or square .

Dip a spatula into some water and smooth the top of the dough. Cool completely, about 1 hour or more. Cut into 3-inch squares. Heat about 1/2-inch of oil in a large skillet.

Use a spatula to lift the squares off the baking sheet.

Fry the Panella 2 to 3 minutes per side until crisp and golden.

Transfer Panella to a paper-towel lined plate to drain.

Squeeze lemon and sprinkle with extra coarse salt, if desired, and serve.

This is one version and I feel it is the simplest. And they are addictive!

Fiori di Zucca Fritta
Fried Zucchini Blossoms

1 cup milk
5 to 6 heaping tablespoons flour (more if needed)
An egg, lightly beaten
Salt, pepper to taste
Chopped basil, parsley, or garlic (optional)
Vegetable oil for frying

Trim the stems of the zucchini blossoms, remove the pistils, wash wash flowers gently and pat them dry just as gently as you can.
Prepare the batter by combining the milk, flour, salt, and egg. (It should be like a light pancake batter add flour if needed)
Heat the oil.
Lightly dredge the zucchini blossoms in the batter, fry them until golden, drain them on absorbent paper, and serve them hot.

You have not lived until you have eaten fried zucchini flowers! They are fit for the Gods.
You can do other things with fried zucchini blossoms too. In Rome I have had them with a small piece of anchovy and a piece of mozzarella tucked inside before frying. You can even use a simple batter made of flour and water with a little salt and pepper.

Panzanella
Bread Salad

Stale bread or hard savory Italian biscuits broken and sprinkled with
water (I like to leave some crunch)
Tomatoes cut (optional)
Garlic chopped
Red onion sliced thin (optional)
Extra virgin olive oil
Coarse salt and freshly ground pepper to taste
Dried Oregano or fresh herbs to taste

This salad features stale bread or hard biscuits which have being
moistened by bein sprinkled or quickly pre-soaked with water. This
salad is most commonly found around the area of Tuscany, where it
is served as a summer salad, featuring garden-fresh ingredients like
tomatoes. Panzanella is quite easy to make. Any number of things
can be added to the salad to make it more interesting or to take
advantage of locally available ingredients.

*A very basic panzanella includes bread, tomatoes, and basil dressed with a
mixture of oil, vinegar (optional), salt, and pepper. I also like to add garlic or
sweet onions, fresh herbs). Any additions should be kept fairly simple for a
more traditional version of the salad.*

Fritto Misto di Mare
Mixed Seafood Fry

1-1/2 cups semolina flour
Coarse salt and freshly ground black pepper
milk or light egg wash (e.g. 1 egg with milk or water)
Vegetable oil for frying
Whitebait or smelts, cleaned
Squid, cleaned and cut into 1" rings
Shrimp, peeled and deveined
A white fish fillets (e.g. cod, cut in cubes)
Parsley chopped
2 lemons, cut in wedges

Mix flour in a medium bowl, season with salt and pepper. In a separate bowl add milk or light egg wash.
Heat about 3" oil in a deep skillet over medium-high heat. Dip fish in milk, a few pieces at a time, and dredge in flour. Repeat process, dipping fish first in milk, then in flour.
Shake excess flour from fish and seafood, and then fry in batches, turning occasionally, until crisp and golden, about 3 minutes. Drain on paper towels, sprinkle with salt, and then transfer to a large platter. Garnish with parsley and serve with lemon wedges.

Fried assorted seafood is a popular appetizer or can be a second dish. It is served every ware in Italy, especially on the southern coasts.

Pasta

Fresh Pasta

Pasta con Uova-Basic Egg Pasta

Impasto di Spinaci-Spinach Pasta

Pici

Trofie

Gnocchi

Cavatelli I II

Tortellini

Ravioli

Crespelli

Manicotti

Pasta con Uova
Basic Egg Pasta

About 2 cups unbleached all-purpose flour; more for dusting
1 cup semolina flour
4 large eggs or 4 -5 medium
1or 2 tablespoon olive oil
A little water if needed

To make the dough the traditional way, combine 2 cups all-purpose flour, the semolina flour, in a mound on a work surface. Make a well in the center of the flour and break the eggs and oil into the well. Beat the eggs with a fork. Then, using the fork, gradually incorporate the flour from the inside walls of the well. When the dough becomes too firm to mix with the fork, knead it with your hands, incorporating just enough of the flour to make soft but dry dough. If the dough needs moisture you can add a very small amount of water. Brush the excess flour aside and knead the dough, adding additional flour as necessary, for about 10 minutes or until smooth. Cover and let rest for 30 minutes or longer.

Cut the dough into 4 pieces. Work with 1 piece at a time, keeping the remaining dough covered. Roll the dough out on a floured surface as thin as possible or use a pasta machine to roll the dough out. Start at the largest setting and keep turning down to the second to the last as the thinnest setting may be too thin. Place on a floured surface and dry slightly, about 5 to ten minutes.

If cutting the pasta by hand, roll up each sheet very loosely and floured like a jelly roll, and then cut it into fettuccine, vermicelli, or lasagna strips with a sharp knife. You may cut the pasta into the desired width with the attachment on the pasta machine. Hang or spread on floured towels, then cook at once or dry for storage.

Cook the pasta in a large pot of boiling water until al dente, 2 to 3 minutes. Drain, sauce, and serve.

Impasto di Spinaci

Spinach Pasta

1/2 cup spinach, fresh or frozen (puréed)
2 to 4 eggs
1 cup semolina flour
3 cups all-purpose flour, plus more as needed
1 teaspoon salt
1 tablespoon olive oil

Squeeze as much water as possible from the chopped spinach. Then in a blender or food processor, combine spinach, eggs, and oil. Puree until the mixture is dark green and smooth, with no chunks of spinach.

Mix flour and salt, stirring to combine. On a work surface pour the flour mixture into a mound. Make a well in the middle. Pour the spinach-egg-oil mixture into the well and, using a fork, then your fingers when the mixture gets too thick, stir more of the spinach mixture in a circular motion, gradually incorporating more and more flour. As the mixture turns thicker, begin to knead it, incorporating enough flour to make dough. Knead dough for about 5 minutes or more, adding more flour until dough is smooth but not sticky. Set aside, covered with plastic wrap, for at least 1 hour or overnight. Divide dough into four to six equal sections and keep all sections but the one you are working with covered. Knead a part of dough a few times by forming it by hand into a flat rectangle, feeding it though the pasta maker at the first (widest) setting, then folding it like a letter and feeding it through the pasta rollers again. Repeat several times at the widest setting, before rolling pasta at increasingly smaller settings until it reaches the desired thinness.

Use sheets of pasta as-is for lasagna, ravioli, or cut into noodles.

Adding pureed spinach turns pasta dough a brilliant green. This pasta dough can be made into linguini, spaghetti, lasagna, or ravioli. It is especially good for Paglia e Fieno (straw and hay).

Pici

Little ones (pici=piccoli=small)

2 cups all-purpose flour
2 cups semolina flour
1 1/4 cups tepid water

Place both types of flour in a large mixing bowl and stir to mix well. Make a well in the center of the flour mixture and add the water a little at a time, stirring with your hands until dough is formed. You may need more or less water, depending on the humidity.

Place the dough on a floured work surface and knead it like bread until smooth and elastic, about 8 to 10 minutes. Cover the dough and let it stand for 30 minutes or more at room temperature.

Roll the dough into long thin dowels about 1/8 to 1/4-inch thick and 6 to 8 inches long . Place the pasta pieces between 2 hands or roll on a board and lightly roll back and forth to create a lightly spiraled and twisted, snakelike noodle. Place the pici on a sheet tray that has been dusted with semolina flour, cover the pasta with a clean dish towel, and set aside until ready to use. At this point, the pasta can be frozen for several months.

Trofie

Thin twisted pasta

Pieces of pasta that have been rolled on a flat surface until it forms a rounded length (1 to 1 1/2 inch) of pasta that has tapered ends are called Trofie. It is then twisted into its final shape. A thin stick can also be used to wrap the pasta length around to aid in forming the twisted shape.

This pasta dough can be used to make all kinds of pasta with no eggs.
I add a little olive oil - 1 to 2 tablespoons.

Gnocchi

Potato Dumplings

2 pounds (about 3) russet potatoes
1 teaspoon salt
1 1/2 cups flour, plus extra
1/2 cup semolina
1 egg
1/8 teaspoon nutmeg (optional)

In a large pot over high heat, combine the potatoes with enough cold water to cover and bring to a boil. Add salt and cook the potatoes, skin on, for about 20 minutes, or until tender when pierced with a knife. Peel them and mash them while they are still hot (a potato ricer works very well here). Season the potatoes with a pinch of salt when cooled, add egg, and slowly knead in enough flour to obtain a firm, smooth, non-sticky dough — exactly how much flour will depend upon how moist the potatoes are. (too soft not enough flour - too hard too much flour). Let the dough rest for about 30 minutes or longer.
Take a small portion of the dough and roll out into snakes about as thick as your finger; cut the snakes into 3/4 to 1-inch pieces and gently score the pieces crosswise with a fork. As an alternative to scoring with a fork you can create a depression on one side. The choice is up to you. Cook the gnocchi in salted boiling water until they float, about 2 to 3 minutes, removing them with a slotted spoon a minute or two after they rise to the surface. Drain them well.

Serve them with a butter sage sauce, melted unsalted butter and parmigiano, meat sauce, pomarola, or pesto.
For gnocchi Sorentino, place gnocchi in baking dish or small individual terrines. Cover with tomato sauce, grated cheese, and plenty of mozzarella. Bake 10 to 15 minutes at 350 F. Top with fresh basil.

I Remember as a child at my Aunt Dolly's house feasting on her homemade gnocchi, her specialty.

Cavatelli

Little Caves

2 1/2 cups fine durum semolina flour
3/4 cup warm water (approximately)
1/2 teaspoon salt
1 tablespoon olive oil

Make a well with the flour, add the water and make a dough. Add
more flour or water as needed.

Knead the dough until smooth like bread dough. Rest the dough
covered for 30 minutes or more then cut dough into pieces and roll
under the palm of your hand to create a log that is the thickness of
your finger and 12 inches long.

Coat each log well in flour to prevent them from sticking as you feed
them through the cavatelli rollers. As they form, place them on
floured towels in single layers.

To make them by hand cut each log into 1/2 to 3/4-inch pieces

With your thumb draw each piece of dough across the tines of a fork
leaving it with an indentation and place as above on floured surface.

*You can buy a cavatelli machine and it is not expensive ; worth the investment
and it is fun to use.*

Cavatelli con Ricotta
Cavatelli made with Ricotta

1 to 1 1/2-pounds of Ricotta cheese
1 to 2 eggs
2 1/2 cups of flour

Beat the eggs lightly together than add the ricotta cheese and flour.
Gently with your hands, mix all the ingredients until they are well
incorporated. Add flour if you need it. Let rest for 30 minutes or
more. Roll the dough onto a lightly floured board, shaping the dough
into small ropes. Cut them into little pieces. Roll them across a
cavatelli/gnocchi board or use the tip of a floured fork tine to form
ridges. Place the Cavatelli on a floured sheet pan and place them into
the freezer. When ready to use, place in a pot of boiling salted water.

Spread them on a cookie sheet and put them in the freezer.
They freeze so well just gather them up after they are frozen place them in a
plastic bag and return them to the freezer.

Tortellini

The pasta
3 1/2 cups flour, plus extra
4 eggs, beaten
Salt

Prepare the pasta: On a flat work surface, mound the flour. Make a well in the center and add the eggs and a pinch of salt. Work the eggs into the flour until dough forms. Form the mixture into a ball, and knead for 10 minutes, adding more flour if necessary. Wrap in plastic and set aside for 30 minutes or more.

Using a pasta machine, roll out the dough until you reach the second-thinnest setting. Cut the pasta sheets into 1 1/2-inch squares or rounds with glass or a ravioli cutter. Place 1/2 teaspoon of filling in the center of each square. Brush the edges of the square with water, and then fold in half or opposite corners over to form a triangle. Press to seal the edges, then bring the opposite corners together, and pinch to form tortellini. As you make them, arrange them on a floured surface so they do not stick together.

The filling
1 1/2 tablespoons butter
4 ounces pork loin, diced
2 ounces chicken breast, diced
4 ounces prosciutto, diced
4 ounces mortadella, diced
1 egg
1/2 cup Italian cheese, freshly grated or more to taste, plus extra
Nutmeg, freshly grated
Salt and freshly ground pepper

In a large skillet over medium heat, warm the butter. Add the pork loin and chicken breast, and sauté until cooked through, about 10 minutes. Let cool. Place the pork, turkey, prosciutto and mortadella in a food processor, and process until well-mixed but still slightly grainy. Place in a bowl, and add the egg, grated cheese, and a pinch of nutmeg. salt and pepper to taste and mix well by hand and set aside. (The filling can be made a day ahead, covered well and kept in the refrigerator.)

Tortellini in Brodo

6 cups meat or vegetable stock

In a large pot, bring the stock to a boil. Season the stock with salt and pepper, add the tortellini, and cook until done, about 2 minutes. Ladle the tortellini and some stock into soup bowls, and sprinkle with Grated cheese.

Homemade Pasta

One of the most rewarding things you can do in Italian cooking is to make fresh pasta though it's often easier to buy pasta in a store; there is something special about making it from scratch at home. While the time and the effort involved are well worth it, it is not all that difficult and you will be generously rewarded for the extra work. Fresh pasta is not a replacement for the dried, factory produced pasta you find on the supermarket shelves. They each have a unique texture and consistency and work better with particular types of sauce. You are really missing out if you limit yourself to dried pasta. Good fresh pasta is much lighter in your mouth and absorbs sauces, especially pasta made with simple ingredients.
Once kneaded, fresh pasta can be made into several shapes including stuffed pastas using one of two methods- rolling out the dough by hand using a wooden rolling pin or passing it through the rollers of a pasta machine.

Ravioli

For the dough
3 1/2 cups flour, plus extra
4 eggs beaten
1/8 teaspoon salt
2 teaspoons olive oil

Prepare the dough on a clean flat surface, Mound the flour, and make a well in the center. Beat eggs and oil slightly in a bowl. Pour the eggs into the well and add the salt. Using a fork or your fingers, work the flour into the eggs until combined. Knead 10 minutes or until a soft smooth dough forms. Wrap the dough in plastic and let rest for at

least 30 minutes or longer. Cut the dough into 4 equal pieces. Work one piece at a time, and cover the other pieces with plastic so they do not dry out. Pass each piece of dough through a pasta machine until it comes together. About 1/16-inch-thick and 4 inches wide and 8 to 10 inches long. Lay the sheet on a flat work surface place1 teaspoon of the filling in the center 1 inch apart over half of pasta sheet. Brush around filling with water to moisten. Fold sheet over; press down to seal. Cut into rounds or squares with round cutter a glass or pastry wheel. Making sure the edges are sealed. Repeat with remaining dough and filling. As you make the ravioli spread them out on a floured surface, so they do not stick together.

Cheese Filling
1 (8 ounce) container ricotta
4-ounce mozzarella cheese, shredded or diced small
1/4 cup Parmigiano grated
1 egg
1/2 tablespoon fresh parsley or basil, chopped
Pinch of nutmeg / Salt and pepper

Combine ingredients in a bowl. Fill rounds of ravioli dough. Serve with your favorite sauce. Use the recipe for cheese ravioli and add 1 cup chopped fresh spinach or frozen spinach that has been cook and squeezed dried.

Meat Filling
1/2-pound meat chopped (e.g.: veal. beef, pork)
1 tablespoon butter
1 1/2 tablespoons onion, finely chopped (optional)
Salt and pepper
1/2 cup Ricotta
1/3 cup Parmigiano
1 egg yolk
Pinch of nutmeg

Sauté onion in butter over medium heat for 1 to 2 minutes. Add meat and cook until meat loses its red or pink color. Transfer to a food processor and pulse a few times to chop. Do not allow it to purée. Put mixture in a bowl and add remaining ingredients. Combine well and fill the ravioli.

Of course, with the filling, you can be as creative as you like. Ravioli can be filled with anything: ricotta, mushrooms, lobster, etc.

Now you are ready to start filling and creating the ravioli

Put the thin sheet of dough on the wooden board and put 1 tsp of filling on the dough about 1" apart.Fold the dough over the filling and cut around it with a ravioli cutter or a form that you may have. Put any excess dough with the rest of the dough and continue the process until you have no more dough.

The finished ravioli can be served with any sauce or Ragu. They are a staple of traditional Italian home cooking.

Crespelle

Pasta Crepes

4 eggs
2 cups all-purpose flour
1 to 1 1/4 cups water
1 cup milk
1/4 tsp. salt
Vegetable oil or melted butter (about 1/4 cup) for cooking the crepes

In mixing bowl, beat eggs with a whisk. Combine milk and water and stir into eggs with whisk. Add the flour gradually, while stirring with the whisk. The batter should be smooth and thin Add water if the batter seems thicker than heavy cream. Add salt; stir.
Set the batter aside to rest for at least 30 minutes.

The Crepes

Heat a 7 or 8-inch crepe pan or small nonstick skillet over medium-high heat. Brush lightly with melted butter or oil Add about 3 tablespoons of batter (I use a large ladle and fill it half way.) As soon as the batter is in the pan, swirl and tilt the pan until the batter coats the bottom of the pan with a thin layer. Work quickly doing this so the batter spreads out before it starts to cook. Once you get the knack of doing this, the rest should be easy!
Cook on one side for about 30 seconds or until set, then turn the crepe over using a spatula or, what I do, is grab it with my finger tips and flip it over...cook the other side just a few seconds. Crepes are made one at a time, brushing the skillet lightly with melted butter before each is made. Slide out of pan, onto a plate, and stack with wax paper between them if they stick. And don't worry if you have to throw out the first two or three crepes before you get them right. Crespelle can be made one or two days in advance and refrigerated, or frozen and kept for weeks. I always like to have some available and ready to use.
Crespelle or Italian crepe can be used in many wonderful Italian dishes. I use them in baked pasta dishes; they can be rolled, stuffed, stacked, or folded.
For classic dishes, like lasagna or for manicotti and cannelloni that require stuffing, these dishes become so light, tender, creamy and delicious! You will love the difference!

Meat Filling for Crepes

1 1/2 tablespoons butter
4 ounces pork loin, diced
2 ounces chicken breast, diced
4 ounces prosciutto, diced
4 ounces mortadella, diced
1 egg
½ cup Italian cheese, freshly grated or more to taste, plus extra
Nutmeg, freshly grated
Salt and freshly ground pepper
meat or vegetable stock to moisten

In a large skillet over medium heat, warm the butter. Add the pork loin and chicken breast, and sauté until cooked through, about 10 minutes. Let cool. Place the pork, prosciutto and mortadella in a food processor, and process until well-mixed but still slightly grainy. Place in a bowl, and add the egg, grated cheese, and a pinch of nutmeg. Salt and pepper to taste and mix well by hand and set aside. (The filling can be made a day ahead, covered well and kept in the refrigerator.)

Manicotti

Prepared pasta dough
Divide dough in half and roll out each half very thin. Cut into rectangles 4 by 5 inches. Let dry for one hour. Into eight quarts of rapidly boiling salted water cook rectangles for 10 to 12 minutes. Drain and cool with a little cold water. Blend all ingredients of filling together. choose the filling of your choice Spread a tablespoon or more of filling on each rectangle. Roll and close. In a baking dish place a little sauce on the bottom add filled manicotti side by side, cover with tomato sauce (even Béchamel) and grated cheese. Bake in hot oven for 15 to 20 minutes.

Prima Piatti

Prima Piatti

Pasta

Salsa Marinara I II
Pomarola
Sugo di Carne Ragu
Bolognese Sauce
Penne Arrabbiata
Pasta all'Amatriciana
Pasta alla Puttanesca
Spaghetti alla Gricia
Lasagna al Forno
Penne Rose
Fetttuccine con Fungi
Paglia e Fieno
Pasta alla Carbonara
Pasta Aglio e Olio
Pasta con Prosciutto e Piselli
Linguini Fini with Anchovies
Orecchiette con Cime di Rapa
Trofe con PestoPasta Primavera
Crespelli Fiorentino
Pasta alla Norma
Cannelloni I II
Gnocchi alla Sorrentina
Pasta Ricotta
Salsa di Besciamell
Burro e' Salvia
Pesto Sauce

Salsa Marinara
Marinara Sauce I

1 small onion, minced
2 garlic cloves, minced
1/4 cup olive oil
2 pounds ripe tomatoes (blanched, peeled and chopped)
Salt & red pepper flakes to taste

In a medium-large saucepan over medium heat, cook the onion and garlic in the oil, stirring occasionally, for about two minutes do not brown.
 Stir in the tomatoes, and salt and pepper, and simmer, covered, stirring occasionally, for 25 minutes. If you like it smooth, Purée the mixture return to a saucepan Simmer the puree, stirring occasionally, for 15 minutes. Makes about 3 cups.

This is one of the most basic and most popular sauces. The flavor is pure and clean and is used with any number of pastas and seafood dishes, Marinara Sauce (Sauce of the Fisherman), if you cannot find very ripe fresh tomatoes, use two (28-ounce) cans peeled whole San Marzano tomatoes.

Salsa Marinara
Marinara Sauce II

1/4 cup of olive oil
4 cloves of garlic sliced in half
1 28 oz can imported Italian plum tomatoes
3 fresh basil leaves, washed, patted dry and chopped
Coarse salt and red pepper flakes to taste

Put the olive oil and the garlic in a large skillet over a medium-high heat and cook until the garlic begins to sizzle but does not brown. Crush and add the tomatoes and cook over a medium-high heat until the tomatoes have reduced, about 15 minutes depending upon your skillet size. Season with salt.
When the sauce has reduced, add the torm basil leaves and the red pepper flakes. Cook for 1-2 minutes, and then remove from the heat.

When the pasta is cooked al dente, drain, and toss with the sauce in the skillet.

You can serve this sauce with spaghetti, (thin spaghetti), or penne. Cheese is not usually recommended, the sauce has such a delicate taste and always recommended for a lighter homemade pasta such as gnocchi, cavatelli, ravioli etc. It is always your choice.
While the sauce is cooking bring 4 quarts of water to a boil in a large pot, add 1 tablespoon of salt, and drop in the pasta all at once, stirring until the pasta is submerged. Cook until al Dente, sauce and serve.

Pomarola

Tuscan Pomarola Sauce

2 cans whole tomatoes, preferably San Marzano
1 stalk celery, chopped small
1 small onion, diced fine
2 cloves garlic (optional)
1 medium carrot, chopped
1 tablespoon extra-virgin olive oil, or to taste
Salt and red pepper flakes, to taste
Fresh basil to garnish

Heat a saucepan with some olive oil and then sauté the vegetables until soft and translucent.

Drain juice from the canned tomatoes into a saucepan. Crush whole tomatoes with your hands as you add them to the pot, along with the celery, onion, and carrot.

Simmer uncovered, until vegetables are soft, and sauce has reduced to about half the volume, about half an hour. Stir occasionally with a wooden spoon, crushing any big lumps of tomato up against the side of the pan. Add a little bit of extra water if the Pomarola sauce seems to be cooking down too quickly. Remove sauce from the heat and add a drizzle of olive oil. Do not cook the olive oil. If you want a smoother sauce, you can run the Pomarola through a food mill or use a stick blender right in the pot, do this before you add the olive oil. Add fresh basel and serve.

A great sauce to serve over rice it was one of my grandmother's favorite.

Sugo di Carne Ragu
Meat Sauce

Soffritto
1 red onion
1 carrot
1 celery stalk

1/2-pound ground beef
1 to 2 sausages, casing removed
1 28 ounce can Italian plum tomatoes (crushed)
1/2 cup red wine
extra virgin olive oil
Coarse salt, red pepper flakes to taste

Finely chop the carrot, onion, and celery.
Place in a pot and sauté in extra virgin olive oil until translucent.
Add the sausage and beef crush to break up the meat and cook.
Raise the heat and stir until almost browned. Add the wine and let the
wine evaporate. Add the tomatoes. Salt and pepper to taste.
Lower the heat and let cook for 45 minutes, stirring occasionally.
If the sauce seems too dry, add some water. and continue cooking.
Great on large pasta Pappardelle, Rigatoni and you can add mushrooms
to give it a great woodsy taste.

This meat sauce is also used for the lasagna and other baked pastas. Ragu, (sugo
di carne) is mostly beef and very little tomato sauce.
Serve with Parmesan on the side.

Sugo Alla Bolognese
Bolognese Sauce

12 ounces ground beef (or beef pork veal)
2 ounces pancetta, minced (optional)
1 1/2 tablespoons olive oil
A quarter of a medium-sized onion, minced
A half a carrot, minced
A six-inch stalk of celery, minced
1/2 cup dry red wine
1 cup crushed tomatoes
Beef, water or even chicken broth
Coarse salt and fresh ground pepper to taste

Mince the vegetables and sauté them with the oil. When the onion is golden not browed, add the ground meat and continue cooking till it is browned. Stir in the wine and let the sauce simmer till the wine has evaporated, then add the tomatoes, a ladle of broth or water, and check the seasoning. Continue simmering over a very low flame for about 1 hour, stirring occasionally, and adding more broth if the sauce looks like it is drying out.

The sauce will improve steadily as it cooks, and if you have the time simmer it longer be simmered for 3 hours, adding boiling water or broth, as necessary. When it is done it should be rich and thick. This sauce invites creativity. You may want to add a few fresh chopped mushrooms or dried porcini (soak them in boiling water first and strain and add the liquid as well), you can add some sausage meat. Use the sauce for pasta (e.g. Rigatoni or Pappardelle) served with Grated Italian cheese.

This is a simple version of Bolognese Sauce just cook it long and slow and the meat will be very tender you can add more wine if you wish but honestly, I prefer my extra wine on the side).

Penne Arrabbiata
"Angry Sauce"

1-pound penne or pasta of your choice
4 tablespoons extra-virgin olive oil
Pancetta to taste (optional)
1 teaspoon dried red pepper flakes or to taste
6 cloves garlic, diced
diced onion (optional
chopped fresh parsley
1 (28 oz.) cans chopped tomatoes with juice
Salt, to taste
Grated Parmesan cheese, if desired

In a large skillet, combine olive oil, (pancetta) red chili flakes, garlic, onion, and parsley. Cook on medium for 3 minutes. Add tomatoes, bring mixture to a boil, and then reduce heat and simmer, covered, for 20 minutes. Salt to taste.
When penne are almost done, reserve 1/3 cup cooking water. Drain penne and add to the sauce with the reserved water. Stir well to combine and cook until water is almost evaporated.

This sauce should be very spicy. Top with grated Parmesan cheese, if desired.

Pasta all' Amatriciana
Pasta Amatriciana

1-pound Bucatini or spaghetti
1/4-pound pancetta or guanciale
1/4-pound ripe tomatoes, chopped or caned plum
Half a small onion, minced
Red pepper flakes to taste
1/2 cup olive oil
An abundance of freshly grated Pecorino Romano

Heat the oil in a skillet, add the diced meat, and cook until it browns,
Add the onion to the grease in the pan, together with the hot pepper,
and when it begins to be translucent add the tomato pieces . Cook,
stirring, for 5-6 minutes, heat it through. Drain the pasta while it is
still a little al dente, add to skillet with the sauce, cook a minute
more, stirring the pasta to coat the strands, add some pasta water if
needed and serve, with grated pecorino.

*Italians traditionally make Amatriciana sauce with Guanciale, salt-cured pork
jowl. It is like flat pancetta, but not as lean, and therefore has a richer feel to it.
If you can find guanciale, use pancetta.*

Pasta alla Puttanesca
Pasta Prostitute Style

1/4 cup extra-virgin olive oil
2 garlic cloves, minced
1/2 teaspoon red pepper flake
4 anchovy fillets
1 (28-ounce) caned whole tomatoes, preferably San Marzano,
chopped
1/2 cup pitted oil cured black olives, roughly chopped
1 to 2 tablespoons rinsed capers
1-pound Bucatini or Linguini Fini

Bring a large saucepan of salted water to boil.
Heat oil add garlic and pepper in a large skillet over medium heat until warm. Add anchovies and continue to heat, breaking up anchovies with a fork. Add tomatoes and stir to combine. Add olives, capers; reduce heat to medium-low and simmer, stirring occasionally, until sauce is thickened, about 8 minutes.
Meanwhile, cook pasta until al dente. Drain pasta and return to pot. Immediately add sauce and stir to combine; warm over low heat, tossing, until sauce coats pasta well, about 1 minute. Sprinkle with chopped parsley.

The word puttanesca is derived from puttana, a colloquial term for 'prostitute.'
Some claim that the sauce earned its name because of its spicy flavor. Another
theory holds that it got its name because it cooks quickly—even women with a
very busy work schedule could prepare it.
Whatever, it is good.

Spaghetti Alla Gricia
Roman Style

1/4 cup extra virgin olive oil
4 ounces pancetta or guanciale, cut into1/4-inch slices, then chopped
coarsely
1/4 teaspoon freshly ground black pepper
1-pound spaghetti
1 cup freshly grated Pecorino Romano cheese

Heat the olive oil in a large sauté pan over medium heat. Add the
guanciale and the hot pepper and sauté until guanciale is crisp.
Remove from the heat.
Bring a large pot of liberally salted water to a boil. Add the spaghetti
and cook uncovered over high heat until al dente.
Place the pan with the guanciale back over medium heat for a few
minutes. Drain the pasta and add it to the pan then remove from heat
an then 1/2 cup of the Pecorino Romano. Stir the pasta vigorously
until guanciale and cheese are well distributed. Add some pasta
water if needed. Serve at once with remaining Pecorino Romano on
the side and an abundant amount of ground black pepper.

*In Italy they would never call this alla Gricia if it was made with Pancetta, only
if it was made with Guanciale.*

Lasagna al Forno

Baked Lasagna

Lasagna noodles or homemade pasta cut into lasagna style shapes
ricotta cheese
shredded mozzarella cheese
grated Romano cheese
1 to 2 eggs
Fresh chopped parsley or Basil
tomato sauce
9x13 baking dish or dish to accommodate at least 3 or 4 layers

Preheat oven 375 F.
In a large pan cook the noodles according to the package instructions. Do not overcook the noodles, if anything under cook a couple of minutes.
Meanwhile in a separate large bowl mix the parsley, ricotta, egg and mozzarella cheese, and Romano cheese.
When noodles are done drain and rinse with cool water to prevent any further cooking.
In 9x13 baking dish spread a layer of sauce.
Lay a layer of noodles, then sauce, then cheese mixture. Repeat ending with a layer of noodles and top with sauce making sure to cover all exposed noodles.
Cover with foil and bake for 35 - 45 minutes until heated through and sauce is bubbling from below.
Sprinkle more mozzarella cheese on top and bake for 5 or 10 minutes until cheese is melted. Let cool for about 10 minutes before serving.

This is basic, use ingredients quantities as desired.
You can also put some cooked meat mixture (Sausage, Ground Beef etc.) or go meatless by layering spinach (cooked and drained well) sautéed zucchini, eggplant or anything else you like. In Italy they even put pieces of chopped hard-boiled egg.

Penne Rosé
Pasta with Creamy Tomato Sauce

1/2 to 1 cup homemade Tomato Sauce (Marinara or Parmarola)
1/2 to 1 cup light cream
small diced onion or a
small clove of garlic (Optional)
Salt and pepper to taste
1/4 cup grated Parmigianino
A scant pound penne
Reserve 1/2 cup pasta water

Bring the water to a rolling boil, salt it, and add the penne.
Meanwhile, heat the tomato sauce and garlic in a saucepan.
When the sauce starts to boil, stir in the cream and heat through,
being careful not to let the sauce boil or it will burn or curdle. Season
to taste and turn off the heat.
When the pasta's cooked, drain it and transfer the penne to a skillet.
Toss or stir for a minute or two with the sauce over medium heat
before serving . You may need a couple of tablespoons of pasta
water to thin the sauce. add plenty of grated cheese and serve.

*Rose' is the original Sauce. Probably a tipsy Italian spilled some vodka into the
sauce while making it and. "WOW! " Penne alla Vodka.
For Vodka Sauce Add 2 oz Vodka when cooking the sauce.*

Fettuccine con Funghi
Fresh Fettuccine with Mushrooms

1 batch fresh pasta (about 1 pound), cut into 1/4-inch wide ribbons
4 ounces dried Porcini mushrooms*
1 cup hot water
2 tablespoons extra-virgin olive oil
2 tablespoons butter
2 clove garlic, thinly sliced or small onion or both
4 ounces prosciutto, chopped or pancetta
1 cup frozen peas, partly thawed (optional)
2/3 to 1 cup light cream
Coarse salt to taste
Fresh ground black pepper to taste
1/2 cup freshly grated Parmigiano-Reggiano

In a small bowl, combine the mushrooms and hot water. Let sit for 30 minutes or until slightly tender, chop, drain and reserve water. Cook
the pasta in a pot of boiling water until tender yet firm to the bite, about 4 minutes.
In a large skillet, combine olive oil, butter, garlic or onion and prosciutto or pancetta and cook on medium-low about 5 to 8 minutes. Add the mushrooms and reserved water. Bring to a boil, then reduce heat and simmer until liquid is mostly evaporated. Add cream, peas, salt, pepper and cook about 2 minutes. Drain pasta and toss with mushroom mixture and add cheese.

You can add fresh sliced mushrooms e.g. shitake or oyster when you sauté the garlic and onion, I think it gives another dimension to the dish even add some fresh herbs e.g. rosemary or thyme instead of the parsley
*Dried porcini mushrooms are available at Italian markets, specialty foods stores and many supermarkets.

Paglia e Fieno
Straw and Hay

1/2-pound egg pasta Tagliatelli*
1/2-pound spinach pasta Tagliatelli*
1 tablespoon chopped onion
4 tablespoons sweet butter
1 cup light cream
4 oz pancetta (chopped) or chopped prosciutto
1 cup frozen peas (thawed)
1/2 to 1 cup grated parmagiana cheese
Freshly ground black pepper

Cook noodles in salted boiling water until al dente.
While pasta is cooking warm the cream in a small saucepan (do not boil)
In a large skillet sauté the butter with the pancetta until meat is almost crisp add the warmed cream, peas and 1 cup of the grated parmgianna
Stir over medium heat until sauce thickens slightly. Drain the noodles an add to the pan and toss to coat with the sauce.
Do not forget if sauce is too thick add a couple tablespoons of pasta water.
Serve with the grated parmagianna and freshly ground pepper.

This is one of my favorite classic Italian dishes; It makes great presentation and so quick and easy. I love to make it, and it is so good.

*Long, thin, flat strips of Pasta about 1/4 inch wide. "Tagliatelle" is the name used in northern Italy for Fettuccine/Tagliatelli - Hand cut Noodles.

Pasta Alla Carbonara
Coalminers Pasta

1 Pound or less of spaghetti or penne
4 to 8 oz pancetta or guanciale
Olive oil
1/2 cup grated Pecorino Romano
2 to 3 eggs depending on size
1/4 cup light cream (optional)
Salt and Fresh ground black pepper

As soon as the water boils, salt it and add the pasta. Meanwhile, dice the meat, sauté it in a tablespoon of oil till it is well cooked.
While the pasta is cooking, in a bowl lightly beat the eggs with the cheese, pinches of salt and pepper, and the cream, if you are using it.
When the pasta is done, drain it and transfer it at once to a heated bowl. Add the pancetta and pour the egg mixture over the pasta, stirring and toss briskly (the heat of the pasta will cook the eggs.) add a little pasta water if needed.
Serve with more cheese and freshly ground pepper.

Italians would scream, No Cream!!

Pasta Aglio e Olio
Spaghetti with Garlic and Oil

1-2 cloves of garlic, minced, or more to taste
1/4 to 1/2 teaspoon dried Red pepper Flakes, or more to taste
1/3 cup good olive oil
1-pound thin spaghetti (I prefer Linguini Fini)
Grated Parmigiano or Pecorino Romano
1/3 cup pasta cooking water
3 tablespoons chopped fresh parsley leaves
Salt to taste

Bring 6 quarts of lightly salted water to a boil and add the spaghetti. In a large skillet mince the garlic, add the red pepper, and sauté them in the oil until the garlic begins to lightly brown. Turn off the heat (the garlic will continue to brown; you do not want it to overbrown and become bitter).

When the pasta is done, drain it well, transfer into the skillet with the garlic and oil and red pepper, and stir add the pasta water as needed. Serve with fresh parsley grated Parmigiano or Pecorino Romano .

What a wonderful dish. If there is one thing that recalls my memories of Christmas Eve. It is Pasta con Aglio e Olio.

Pasta con Prosciutto e Piselli
Pasta with Prosciutto and Peas

Small shells or Ditalini pasta
Extra virgin olive oil
1/2 medium onion minced (or more to taste)
Prosciutto or pancetta minced (at least 4 oz.)
Frozen petite peas (fresh if you have)
4 cups chicken broth
Salt and red pepper flakes to taste
Freshly grated Pecorino Romano cheese
Fresh chopped parsley (optional)

Cook pasta in a pot of salted boiling water until al dente. Drain and reserve one cup of pasta water. set aside.

Heat oil in another large pot. Stir in minced onion and Prosciutto or pancetta. Sauté till onion is soft.

Add frozen peas and broth and simmer mixture till peas are cooked. Season with salt and pepper if necessary.

When peas are tender, add the cooked pasta to the broth and stir to combine. The mixture should be soupy. Add extra broth or water if mixture is too dry. Finish with a drizzle of extra olive oil and freshly chopped parsley if you like. Season with Pecorino Romano cheese and Red pepper flakes and serve in individual soup bowls.

Pasta Piselli is a perfect blend between a soup and a pasta dish and wonderful comfort food. Hearty and flavorful and delicious.

Linguini alle Acciughe
Linguine with Anchovies

1/3 cup olive oil
2 to 3 cloves garlic chopped
1 can anchovies 2 ounce drained (better yet the kind sold whole in
tins rinsed, boned, and minced)
Abundant minced parsley
Red pepper flakes to taste
1-pound linguini fini or thin spaghetti
a few chopped black cured pitted olives for garnish

Bring a pot of lightly salted water to a boil and add the pasta. While it's cooking sauté the cloves of garlic in the oil in a large skillet (don't let them burn). Add the anchovies, together with a tablespoon or two of the pasta water. Turn off the flame and continue stirring the sauce to dissolve the anchovy filets, season with pepper. As soon as the pasta is done drain and transfer it to the skillet and toss it with the sauce over a low flame for a few seconds. If dry add some more pasta water to create the sauce.

A traditional Neapolitan Christmas Eve dish,

Orecchiette con Cime di Rapa
Orecchiette with Broccoli Rabe

1-pound orecchiette
1 1/4 pounds broccoli rabe
Red pepper flakes to taste
2 to 3 cloves garlic, minced
6 tablespoons olive oil
1/2 cup chicken stock or pasta water
Grated Pecorino Romano

Pick over and clean the broccoli and cut into smaller pieces. Bring a pot of water to a boil, salt it, add the broccoli, and after a few minutes test for tenderness when cooked drain and set aside. In another pot boil the pasta. While the pasta's cooking, simmer the garlic, red pepper and the oil in a skillet taking care that the garlic does not brown and become bitter. Add the broccoli Sauté 1 to 2 minutes. Drain the pasta, then add to the skillet with the oil, garlic and broccoli, cook, stirring, add pasta water if needed for a few seconds to distribute the seasoning evenly, and serve with grated cheese.

With Sausage: 8 ounces sausage casings removed, cook the sausage until browned in a large skillet over medium-high heat, breaking it into 1/2-inch pieces with a wooden spoon, about 3 minutes. Stir in the garlic, red pepper flakes, and 1/2 teaspoon salt. Cook, stirring, until the garlic is fragrant and slightly toasted, about 1 to 2 minutes. Add the broccoli rabe and chicken broth,

With Anchovies: 6 Anchovies (rinsed and bone if salted ones are used). Heat the oil, garlic and pepper in a skillet and add the fish, stirring them vigorously to reduce them to a liquid sauce then add the broccoli then continue.

Orecchiette are a distinctive type of pasta shaped roughly like small ears, hence the name (orecchio, ear, orecchiette, little ears).

Trofie con Pesto
Trofie with Pesto

1/2 pound Trofie pasta
Pesto sauce (Page 79)
1 cup String beans
1 cup Potatoes cubed
1/2 cup Extra Virgin Olive oil
Parmigiano cheese
Salt and pepper to taste

In a large pot of boiling water add the potatoes and the string beans. After a couple of minutes add the Trofie pasta or any other pasta that you prefer. The timing is a little tricky; they all should all cook together.
Once the pasta is cooked "al dente", drain from the pot and put in a serving bowl. Add the Pesto sauce. And a little of the pasta water if needed, Mix well and drizzle with extra virgin olive oil and Parmigiano cheese.

Original Ligurian pesto " Trofie a la Genovese"
the first time I ever had pesto sauce was in Genoa visiting a friend's parents.
My friend Marcello taught me how to make it the way they did with no garlic
and I knew it as, Salsa Verdi -Green Sauce

Pasta Primavera

3/4-pound Linguini Fini pasta or spaghetti
Broccoli, about 1 heaping cup of florets
1 small zucchini, diced
asparagus spears cut to one-inch pieces
1/2 cup peas, fresh or frozen
1/2 cup sliced mushrooms
3 minced garlic cloves chopped
Basil leaves, chopped
4 oz pancetta or prosciutto
4 Tbsp. Extra virgin olive oil
1/4 cup chicken broth or vegetable broth
1/3 cup light cream (optional)
1/2 cup grated parmesan cheese
Salt and fresh ground pepper to taste

Pre-cook the broccoli and asparagus, for about 1-minute in boiling water (do not overcook). Remove the vegetables and plunge them into ice water and drain. and set aside.

In a large sauté pan, heat the oil over medium-high heat, Sauté pancetta until lightly brown, add the garlic and sauté 1 minute. Add the diced zucchini, mushrooms, and peas, sauté another 2 minutes, stirring often. Add blanched vegetables. Pour in the chicken or vegetable broth and turn the heat to high to bring it to a boil. Add the cream If you are using, Stir. Turn the heat down until the chicken broth mixture is just simmering, not boiling. (Vegetables should still be al dente)

Boil the pasta: you will want to start cooking it before you begin sautéing the garlic and vegetables. Linguini or spaghetti can take 8-12 minutes.

When the pasta is done, transfer it with tongs into the sauce and combine. Add the Parmesan cheese and stir. If the sauce seems too thick add some chicken broth, cream, or water.

Add the basil. Add salt if needed. Grind some course black pepper over everything and serve.

69

Crespelli Fiorentino
Florentine Spinach Crepe

Crespelli (page 46)

Filling
4 cups spinach washed, and stems removed
1 1/2 pound ricotta cheese, drained
1 large egg
1 cup mozzarella cheese, shredded
1 medium sweet onion, chopped
1 teaspoon minced garlic
1 tablespoon fresh parsley, chopped
1 teaspoon olive oil
Fresh Nutmeg to taste
Parmagiano to taste
Coarse salt
Fresh ground black pepper

Add spinach to pan and cook until it is lightly wilted. Then, remove spinach from heat and drain juices.

In a large mixing bowl, combine ricotta cheese and egg and mix thoroughly. Then stir in parsley, black pepper, nutmeg, Parmigiano and mozzarella cheese. Mix in spinach.

Preheat oven to 350 F.
 Lightly grease a large pan. Then lay out crepes on plate. Spoon spinach and cheese mixture along the middle of crepe and roll the crepe over. Place each crepe in the pan, side by side.
Top the crepes with tomato, béchamel sauce or both, and shredded mozzarella cheese
Place in oven and cook for approximately 25-30 minutes.
Remove from oven then serve.

You can substitute fresh spinach with frozen spinach. It must be defrosted and drained very well.

Pasta alla Norma
Pasta with Eggplant

2 medium eggplants, peeled and cut into 1/2-inch cubes
Corse salt
1 cup vegetable olive oil
1/4 cup extra virgin olive oil
1 cup chopped onion
4 cloves garlic, minced
1/4 teaspoon red pepper flakes
1 28 ounce can plum tomatoes crushed
1 1/4 cups Ricotta Salata*, freshly grated or (1/2 cup of fresh Ricotta)
Pasta of your choice (perhaps Penne Rigatoni or Buccatini)

Put the eggplant cubes in a colander, sprinkle with kosher salt and let rest for about an hour, Drain the eggplant, pat dry removing any excess salt.

Pour the cup of oil into a large skillet over medium high heat. Place the eggplant in a single layer in the hot oil and try them for about 10 minutes, stirring occasionally until the eggplant is soft and cooked through and browned on all sides. If necessary, work in batches so that the eggplant is not crowded in the skillet. When the eggplant is cooked, remove them from the pan with a slotted spoon onto a plate lined with paper towels to eliminate the excess oil. Keep warm.

In a clean large skillet, heat the olive oil over medium heat. Add the onion, garlic and red pepper flakes and sauté until the onion is soft and translucent, about 5 minutes. Add the tomatoes with their juice. Season to taste with salt and pepper. Cook over low heat for about 20 to 25 minutes or until the sauce is slightly thickened. Simmering over low heat.

Bring a pot of salted water to a boil and add the pasta and cook until al dente. Save some of the cooking water, add the pasta into the tomato sauce. Mix together and remove from the heat.

(If the sauce is dry, add some of the cooking water) Add the torn basil, one cup of ricotta salata and the eggplant chunks. Toss well.

Divide the pasta into individual plates, Sprinkle the remaining ricotta salata on top. Serve.

*Ricotta salata can be found in some food stores and in Italian specialty shops

This majestic pasta was named after Norma, an opera composed by Vincenzo Bellini, who was born in Catania.

Cannelloni di Spinaci e Ricotta
Spinach Ricotta Cannelloni

1 Recipe for pasta dough /or Crespelli
For the Filling
3 Cups Fresh Spinach Leaves Steamed, Drained and Finely Chopped
(Makes about 1/2 to 3/4 Cup Cooked)
2 Cups Ricotta Cheese
1 egg
1/2 Cup Grated Parmesan Cheese
Coarse Salt & Pepper
Dash of Nutmeg
3-4 Tablespoons Finely Chopped Fresh basil or parsley
Topping
2 to 3 Cups Tomato Sauce
1/2 Cup Grated Italian Cheese and 1/2 cup grated mozzarella

If making the pasta from scratch. Prepare the egg pasta following the instructions given, and cut into 8 four and a half inch squares. Cook the pasta sheets in boiling water for just I minute, Cool.
Mix together the ingredients listed for the filling. Preheat an oven to 375 degrees F. Place about 1/3 cup filling into the center of each pasta sheet and roll up into a cylinder. Once all sheets are filled, place about 1 cup of the sauce on the bottom of a 9 x 12-inch pan, and then lay the cannelloni seam down on top of this. Continue forming the cannelloni until they are all assembled in the baking pan. Spread the remaining sauce on top, and then sprinkle with the remaining cheese. Bake until bubbling and golden, about 30 minutes. Let stand 10 minutes before serving. Carefully remove the cannelloni, on to a plate, and serve.

Delicate sheets of egg pasta are stuffed with a ricotta and spinach filling which is then topped with a light, fresh tomato sauce and baked. You can assemble them hours in advance and simply bake before serving. A topping of béchamel sauce is also a great addition.

Cannelloni con Carne
Cannelloni with Meat

1 recipe basic pasta dough or Crespelli Page
1 cup basic tomato sauce Page
1 cup besciamella Page
For the Filling
1-pound mixed Beef, Veal, Pork ground fine
1/2-pound mortadella
1 Cup diced mozzarella
1 Cup grated Parmigiano cheese
1 Onion
1/2 Cup white wine (optional)
Fresh black pepper
Nutmeg
Extra virgin olive oil or butter
Salt

In a large skillet, add 3 Tablespoons of olive oil and the onion finely chopped. Sauté the onion until translucent and add the meat.
Sauté the meat for a few minutes and add the white wine.
Let evaporate. Cook the meat at medium heat until tender, let the meat cool .
Put the meat in a food processor, add the mortadella and pulse.
Pour the content in a bowl; add the mozzarella, Parmigiano cheese, fresh ground black pepper and a dash of nutmeg.
Cover an oven pan with a layer of the tomato sauce. Fill each crepe with about 3 or 4 tablespoons of filling. Fill and roll the crepe.
Arrange the crepe in the pan. Prepare all you Cannelloni to fill the pan.
Cover each crepe with besciamella sauce and dabs of tomato sauce then a generous sprinkle of Parmigiano cheese.
Bake until bubbling and golden, about 20 to 25 minutes at 325 F

Gnocchi alla Sorrentina
Gnocchi Sorrento Style

Gnocchi
Fresh tomato sauce
Mozzarella (cubed)
Parmesan
Fresh Basil leaves.

Boil the gnocchi in boiling salted water, when they come to the surface, drain.

Take a baking dish, pour a tablespoon of sauce on the bottom, and then put the gnocchi, mozzarella, cut into cubes, tomato sauce, parmesan cheese and some basil leaves. Make another layer in the same way.

Put in preheated oven at 350 F degrees for 15 minutes until the Parmesan is well baked.

A typical Neapolitan food, and the best place to have them is on the Amalfi Coast. In Italy Gnocchi are always served on Thursdays. Why ? Don't know.

Pasta Ricotta

Pasta with Ricotta

1-pound penne (any pasta is fine)
2 tablespoons olive oil or unsalted butter, cut into pieces
1 1/2 cup fresh ricotta
1/4 cup roughly chopped parsley
Grated Parmigiano
Oil Cured black pitted olives
Coarse salt to taste
Freshly ground black pepper

Cook the pasta according to the package directions. Reserving 1/3 cup of the water, drain the pasta, then return it to the pot. In a medium bowl, whisk together the butter, ricotta, and pasta water until a rich, creamy sauce forms. Pour the sauce over the hot pasta. Add the parsley, salt, and pepper and toss.

Tip: Ricotta can vary dramatically in taste and texture. Depending on the brand you use, you may need to add extra pasta water and butter to create a sauce that is sufficiently creamy.
Top with grated cheese.
And garnish with a tablespoon chopped Oil Cured Black olives or parsley

Great for children (no olives) or simple first plate. kids loved it.

Salsa di Besciamella

White Sauce

4 cups milk
Salt to taste
8 tablespoons (1 stick) Butter   (unsalted)
1/4 teaspoon fresh grated nutmeg
1/2 cup flour

In a medium saucepan, scald the milk (bring to just under a boil), remove from the heat, and set aside.

In another saucepan, melt the butter over medium-high heat. Add the flour and stir with a wooden spoon until smooth, cooking the paste about 1 minute. Slowly stir in the milk, salt, and nutmeg; cook, stirring, until the mixture comes to soft a boil. Continue stirring until the sauce thickens, about 5 minutes. Remove the sauce from the heat. The sauce is ready to use.

This béchamel, or white sauce, can be used to make lasagna, cannelloni, and Gnocchi Sorrentino.
You can add Gorgonzola cheese to this it will make a different kind of Gorgonzola sauce.

Burro e' Salvia

Butter and Sage Sauce

6 tablespoons unsalted butter
1 tablespoon fresh sage, finely chopped
Salt and pepper

Heat butter in a saucepan over medium heat until it begins to brown. Stir in sage and cook 1-2 minutes.

Season with salt and pepper. Pour over pasta. Add pasta water if neened to thin.

Pesto alla Genovese
Basic Pesto Sauce

Here is a basic Italian recipe that you can use for many dishes! The basic pesto sauce is a classic sauce used in much of Italian cooking. For years, many Italians felt strongly that this sauce should be made by hand, with a pestle and mortar. If you use a food processor you will get similar results. The sauce is served with different types of pasta, as a flavoring for soups, and on a fresh Mozzarella and tomato salad.

1 cloves garlic (I omit the Garlic -if you decide to use it let it
marinate in olive oil for about 1 hour to get the bite out)
1 large bunch Basil leaves (about 2 cups or more) rinsed and dried
1/4 cup pine nuts, walnuts, or both
Coarse Salt to taste
Fresh ground, black pepper
1 cup extra virgin olive oil
1/2 cup Parmesan cheese

Peel and crush the garlic clove. Mince the basil leaves.
Blend garlic, basil, and 1/2 cup olive oil, and cheese in a food processor or blender. Use low speed and stop often to stir. Gently blend in the rest of olive oil and the pine nuts.
Let sit for about 1 hour before using.

Original Genovese Pesto included cooked String beans and boiled potatoes with the pasta (smaller Troffe was used)

Prima Piatti

Polenta

Cooked Corn Meal
Sausages and Polenta
Polenta with Gorgonzola
Fried Polenta

Risotto

Asparagus Risotto
Rise e Bisi
Risotto Milanese
Risotto with Porcini Mushrooms
Seafood Risotto

Polenta

Cooked Corn Meal

4 cups water
1 1/4 teaspoons salt (or to taste)
1 cup yellow cornmeal (medium to fine)
2 tablespoons unsalted butter
1/3 cup finely grated Parmesan cheese (optional)

In a saucepan, combine the water and salt and bring to a boil. Using a wooden spoon, gradually stir in the cornmeal. Reduce heat to medium low and cook, stirring, until the cornmeal is thick and just begins to pull away from the sides of the pan as you stir, 20 to 25 minutes. Stir in the butter and Parmesan cheese. (traditional way)

I add the cornmeal to cold water then heat it to a boil, it reduces the number of lumps. If is too stiff add more water if to thin cook it down to reduce (the more, you cook it the smoother it gets) It takes a little practice to get the rite consistency, but it is worth it.

A popular food in the north of Italy,
Polenta is the traditional main staple. its consumption was traditionally associated with lower classes, it was an essential food in their everyday nutrition.

Polenta con le Salsicce
Sausages and Polenta

A not too firm polenta cooked
3 to 4 sweet Italian link sausages, about a pound in all
1/2 cup tomato sauce
1/2 cup grated Parmigiano
2 tablespoons oil

Preheat oven to 375 F
Cook the polenta. Meanwhile, cook the sausages in another pan with just a drop of water. When they are done, skin and them and break them up, and mix them with the tomato sauce.
Once the polenta is ready, spread it out about a finger thick in an ovenproof dish and sprinkle with the Parmigiano, sausages, and sauce ,drizzle oil. Heat the dish through in the oven . 15 to 20 minutes and serve.

Polenta takes very well to being baked and becomes special if sausages enter the picture. Adding mozzarella as topping and bake 15 to 20 minutes makes it very special.
Especially good in winter.

Polenta con Gorgonzola
Polenta with Gorgonzola

1/2 cup light cream
3 to 4 ounces of Gorgonzola cheese, cut into small cubes
Kosher salt and freshly ground black pepper to taste

When the polenta is done, reduce the heat stirring constantly with a wooden spoon, until polenta thickens and pulls away from the sides of the pot. Make sure it does not burn and stick to the pan. Turn off the heat add cream, Gorgonzola and stir until the cheese melts. Add salt and pepper to taste. Transfer to bowls and serve.

Adding Gorgonzola may not authentic Italian but adding any other kind of cheese is.

Fried Polenta

Cook polenta according to cooking instructions. Pour into a lightly greased, 13 x19 inch baking dish cover and chill 3 to 4 hours.
Cut the polenta into 2 by 4-inch pieces. Heat the oil in a heavy large skillet over medium-high heat. Working in batches, fry the polenta pieces until golden brown on all sides, about 3 minutes per side. Using tongs, transfer the polenta pieces to paper towels and drain. Place the polenta pieces on a baking sheet and keep warm in the oven while cooking the remaining batches.

Polenta Table

A traditional way to serve polenta is very casual, family-style. That does not just mean passing the dishes around, it means just one dish for everyone! What fun! Ok, it is served up on one big board or directly poured on a wooden table for everyone to enjoy. It is really a sight to behold when it is on the table. If you don't have a huge board. Just pick up a large piece of pine at the hardware store and cover it with a layers of parchment paper. If you have never heard of an Italian polenta table, then you've been missing out one of the messiest and most-enjoyable culinary experiences out there, Polenta is poured right onto the large wooden table before getting topped with lots of spicy sauce, meatballs, braciola, sausages, pork ribs, neck bones cooked in sauce. Sautéed broccoli rabe and a plenty of freshly grated Parmesan. Everyone gets forks, knives, spoons and plenty of napkins - proving once and for all that plates are just unnecessary. It is like a show! Splashing Sunday gravy on the table over the polenta, meats and vegetables gives you an experience you never had before. Give a polenta table a try, Fun! Fun! Fun! Delicious food and serve with lots of wine.

Risotto

Risotto is the kind of rice that Italian mostly eat after the Antipasto, as a first plate. A person can choose between Risotto or Pasta, and then follow by a second plate. This tradition of eating Risotto is very common, especially in the northern part of the country, Risotto mostly grown in that region.

Risotto
Making Risotto: The Basics

Making a good risotto it takes time and a little bit of practice, but it is well worth the effort, the rich texture and just-right doneness that a good home-made risotto should have.

The best rice's for making risotto are Arborio and Vialone Nano. other rice will not do.

Almost all risotto are made with the same basic procedure, with minor variations: Begin by mincing a small volume of onion and whatever other herbs the recipe calls for. Sauté the mixture in abundant olive oil or unsalted butter, then stir in the rice and sauté until it becomes translucent (this will take 7-10 minutes), stirring constantly to keep it from sticking. Stir in a third of a cup of dry wine. Once the wine has evaporated completely, add a ladle of simmering broth; stir in the next before all the liquid is absorbed, continue cooking, stirring and adding broth as the rice absorbs it, until the rice barely reaches the al dente stage . Stir in a tablespoon of butter and the grated cheese (if the recipe calls for it), cover the risotto, and turn off the flame. Let it sit, covered, for two to three minutes, and serve.

If you want a richer risotto, stir in a scant quarter cup of lightcream in addition to the butter. Risotto that has had cream stirred into it is remarkably smooth.

Risotto agli Asparagi
Asparagus Risotto

1-pound asparagus
1/2 a small onion, finely sliced
1 1/2 cups short-grained rice (Arborio)
1/4 cup plus 2 tablespoons butter, or
1/4 cup olive oil plus 2 tablespoons butter
1/3 cup dry white wine, warmed
1 cup grated Parmigianino
The water the asparagus was cooked in, with chicken or vegetable
broth to make about1 quart, simmering
Salt and fresh ground pepper

Clean and boil the asparagus for a few minutes , or until a fork easily penetrates the tip of a spear. Remove the asparagus from the water. remove tender tips and cut the stalks into one-inch lengths set them aside.

Sauté the onion in half the butter or the oil, and when its translucent, remove it to a plate with a slotted spoon. Next, stir in the rice and sauté, stirring, until the grains have turned translucent, 5-7 minutes. Stir in the wine and cook until it has evaporated. Then add the asparagus stem to the rice, and begin stirring in the liquid, a ladle full at a time. Continue adding liquid, and when the rice is almost done, stir in half the reserved tips. Check seasoning and continue cooking the rice untill it is al dente. Turn off the heat and stir in the remaining butter and half the grated cheese. Let the risotto stand covered for two minutes, then transfer it to a serving dish and garnish it with the remaining tips. Sprinkle the remaining grated cheese over it and serve.

Asparagus risotto is especially good in the spring, when asparagus is at its freshest.

Risi e Bisi
Rice and Peas Italian Style

5 cups chicken stock
4 Tablespoons olive oil
1/2 cup onion, chopped
2 cups fresh green peas (you may use frozen)
1 1/2 cups Aborio rice
2 Tablespoons unsalted butter
1/2 cup Parmesan cheese, freshly grated
Coarse salt and freshly ground pepper

Bring the chicken stock to a simmer in a medium-large pot, then lower the heat so that the stock continues to barely simmer.
In a skillet heat the 4 Tablespoon of olive oil over medium heat.
Add the onion and cook until it is transparent, but not browned.
Add the peas and rice to the onions. Cook over medium heat for two minutes.
Add two cups of vegetable stock and cook until the liquid is all but absorbed (do not let the rice get dry).
Add another cup of stock and cook, stirring, until the stock is almost absorbed.
Repeat with more stock, only adding 1 cup at a time, until the rice is tender. Stir in the 2 Tablespoons butter, cheese, and serve.

You can add sautéed mushrooms (in butter) if you like, it brings this dish to another level.

Risotto Milanese
Milanese style Rice

2 tablespoons olive oil
6 tablespoons butter
1 medium onion chopped fine
saffron threads to taste
2 cups arborio rice
1/2 cup white wine
4 cups chicken broth
1/2 cup freshly grated Italian cheese

In a heavy bottomed skillet, heat the olive oil and 2 tablespoons of the butter over medium heat. Add the onion and cook until softened and translucent, 8 to 10 minutes. Add the saffron and cook, stirring, for 1 minute. Add the rice and stir with a wooden spoon until the rice is well coated and translucent, 3 to 4 minutes.

Add the wine to the rice, and then add a 4 to 6-ounce ladle of simmering broth and cook, stirring occasionally, making sure all the liquid is absorbed.

Continue adding the stock a ladle at a time, waiting until the liquid is completely absorbed before adding more.

After about 20 minutes begin to taste the rice. It is ready when it is tender and creamy, but still a little firm to the bite.

Stir in the remaining 4 tablespoons of butter and the cheese until well mixed. Transfer to serving plates and serve.

Risotto ai Funghi Porcini
Risotto with Porcini Mushrooms

A one-ounce packet dried porcini
Extra fresh Mushrooms if you like
1/2 of a small onion, chopped fine
1/4 cup plus 2 tablespoons butter, or 3 tablespoons olive oil 1/4 cup
butter
1 1/2 cups rice, Arborio or Vialone Nano
1/3 cup dry white wine
1 cup freshly grated Parmigiano
1/2 cup light cream (optional)
The water the mushrooms were soaked in, strained, and a quart of
simmering water, beef, or chicken broth
A bunch of parsley, minced
Coarse Salt and Fresh ground pepper to taste

Soak the porcini in a cup of hot water for fifteen minutes or until
soft.
Slice the onion finely and sauté it in three tablespoons of oil or 1/4
cup of butter. Add the rice. Sauté the rice for several minutes or until
it becomes translucent, stirring constantly. Add the wine and
continue stirring until it has evaporated completely. Then add a first
ladle of liquid (if you are using plain water, add salt at this time), and
while it is absorbing, chop the mushrooms and strain the liquid they
soaked in. Add the mushrooms and their liquid to the rice, then
continue adding water or broth a ladle at a time, stirring occasionally
About five minutes before the rice is done, check seasoning as soon
as the rice is al dente, turn off the heat, stir in the remaining butter,
half the cheese, the cream if you're using it, a little bit of ground
pepper, the parsley, and cover the risotto for two minutes. Serve with
the remaining grated cheese.

*Mushroom risotto is wonderful, especially in the fall when the mushrooms are
fresh. You can use fresh wild mushrooms. If you have stems, chop them, and for
a special treat a little Truffle Oil.*   91

Risotto a Frutta di Mare
Seafood Risotto

1/2-pound cockles or small clams
1/2-pound mussels
1/2 cup extra--virgin olive oil
1 garlic clove, minced
Red pepper flakes to taste
2 cups short-grain rice (e.g. Arborio)
1/2 cup dry white wine
1 plum tomato, peeled, seeded, and diced (optional)
6 cups fish stock or clam broth
1/4-pound cleaned squid, bodies cut into rings and tentacles halved
1/4 pound medium shrimp, shelled and deveined
1 tablespoon unsalted butter
1 tablespoon minced Italian parsley

In a large bowl, soak the cockles and mussels in water to cover with 1 tablespoon of the salt for 30 minutes. Drain and rinse thoroughly (this is to get rid of sand and purge them). Place the cockles and mussels in a 2 quart pot with 1/2 cup of water and cover with a lid; cook over medium heat until they open, about 8 minutes. Remove from the heat, cool a few minutes, and shell; transfer to a dish discarding the shells and any unopened cockles and mussels. Strain the cooking juices in the pot through cheesecloth-lined sieve into the bowl with the shelled cockles and mussels.

Heat the olive oh in a heavy-bottomed 2-quart sauté pan over a medium-high flame Add the garlic and chili; heat until fragrant, about 30 seconds, stirring constantly with a wooden spoon making sure that the garlic does not burn. Add the rice and cook 3 minutes, stirring constantly, Deglaze with wine. When the wine has evaporated, after about 2 minutes, add the tomato (optional); cook 5 minutes, still stirring.

Heat the broth in a 2-quart saucepan. Add 1/2 cup of the he broth to the rice and cook, stirring, until it is absorbed. Continue to cook the rice, stirring constantly and add broth by the 1/2 cup whenever the liquid has been absorbed, about 15 minutes. Add the cockle's mussels, along with their reserved cooking liquid, then stir in the squid and shrimp; cook until the rice is done (al dente) about 3 more minutes, add broth as needed (too much broth result in soggy rice rather than a creamy risotto), Season the risotto with Coarse salt and freshly ground pepper , add the butter parsley, and serve.

Zuppa

Prima Piatti
Zuppa

Brodo di Pollo

Brodo di Manzo

Tortellini in Brodo

Stracciatella

Pasta e Finocchi

Scarola e Fagioli

Minestrone

Pasta Lenticchia

Zuppa di Salsicce e Pasta

Pasta e Ceci

Pasta e Fagioli

Ribollita

Battuto e Suffrito

How is it that plain chicken and vegetables simmered together can taste so satisfying?
Broth is one of the great inventions of all time. It serves as in ingredient in all sorts of things, a bowl of broth is the perfect supper after a filling midday meal. For that matter, broth with tortellini or cappelletti is a standard first course at festive dinners. A good bowl of broth will warm you in the winter.

Brodo di Pollo

Chicken Broth

1 (3 pound) whole chicken cut up
4 carrots, halved
2 stalks celery
1 large onion
Fresh parsley
2 cloves garlic
Salt and pepper to taste
Enough water to cover

Put the chicken, carrots, celery, and onion in a large soup pot and cover with cold water. Heat and simmer do not boil, uncovered, until the chicken meat falls off the bones (skim off foam every so often). Take everything out of the pot. Strain the broth. Pick the meat off the bones and reserve. Discard the vegetables. Season the broth with salt, pepper to taste, if desired. Return the chicken, chop more fresh carrots, celery, and onion to the pot, stir together and cook for another 20 minutes.

Use the cookrd chicken in a croquet (shredded chicken, bread crumbs, eggs, chopped onion, grated cheese Parsley salt pepper a little water) Make Croquets shape, flour lightly and fry in oil.

One of my grandmother's favorites.

Brodo di Manzo
Beef Broth

2-3 quarts of water
2 pounds of beef, either shanks, ribs, or neck bones
A piece of spongy bone, or a joint, split (optional)
2 sticks of celery
2 carrots
A bunch of fresh parsley
1 onion quartered
A tomato chopped (optional)
3 to 5 peppercorns
2 cloves garlic
Salt to taste

The beef should not be too lean. A piece of marrow, or a joint, split, enriches the broth,
Start with cold water; figure about a quart of water per pound of meat. Add the meat, vegetables, and seasonings to the water at the same time in a pot. Heat the over a high flame until the broth comes to a boil, and then turn the heat down. Simmer the broth for a couple of hours, or until a fork easily penetrates the meat. Check the seasoning, strain the broth, let it cool, and skim the fat that rises to the surface (the best way to do this is to chill the broth and remove the fat with a fork). Use the broth to make soups or serve it by itself. When serving plain broth, most Italians will add a couple of tablespoons of fine pasta such as crumbled vermicelli or pastina to the soup.

Use the Beef as a boiled dinner or for a salad. (Cooked beef, fresh celery, red onion, salt pepper and vinegar and olive oil and let marinate for several hours.) One of my favorites.

Tortellini in Brodo

Tortellini in Broth

8 cups chicken or beef broth
Cheese or meat Tortellini preferably fresh and homemade (6or 8 per person)
2 tablespoons chopped fresh Italian parsley leaves

Heat the broth into a large saucepan. Cover and bring to a slow boil over medium high heat. Add the tortellini. Simmer over medium heat until al dente, about 7 minutes.
Ladle the broth and tortellini into soup bowls. Top with fresh parsley Parmesan and freshly ground black pepper and serve.
Tortellini are fun to make and easy after you learn the procedure.
The filling can either be cheese or meat. You can use market products but if you do buy only the very best.

This is the best of the best - fresh tortellini or tortoloni in broth.

Stracciatella

Italian Egg Drop Soup

About 2 quarts chicken or beef broth
4 eggs
3 tablespoons freshly grated Parmigiano
1 tablespoons semolina (optional)
A pinch of freshly ground nutmeg (optional)
1 tablespoon very finely minced parsley (optional)

In a bowl, combine the eggs, semolina (If you' are including it), grated
cheese, and, nutmeg. Add 2 to 3 tablespoons of broth to the eggs and beat the mixture lightly with a fork.
Bring the broth to a boil. Add the egg mixture in one fell swoop, stirring vigorously with a whisk or fork to break up the egg, which will form fine light flakes, rags (stracci, in Italian) that give the soup its name. Simmer for another 2-3 minutes, stirring constantly, add parsley and serve, with more grated Parmigiano on the side.

For a change you can add some cooked spinach and or small pasta.

Pasta e Finocchio
Fennel Soup

Fennel fronds from one or two fennel bulbs chopped
(Use bulbs to make a salad)
Salt and Red pepper flakes to taste
1-quart water or Chicken Stock
2 to 3 tablespoons extra virgin olive oil
1 to 2 cloves garlic chopped
1 small onion chopped (optional
2 cups plum tomatoes diced or broken up with your hands
1 to 1 1/2 cup Pasta (spaghetti) broken into 1-inch pieces

Wash and then cut fennel fronds into small pieces. Boil fennel fronds in 1 quart lightly salted water or stock until tender; this is your soup base.
In a pot Sauté garlic and onion in olive oil (do not brown) add tomatoes sauté for 10 minutes season with red pepper flakes to taste. Then add cooked fennel and water. Add broken pasta (spaghetti) and Cook until pasta is done add more water or stock as needed it should not be too thin but soupy, adjust seasonings and serve.

This is a great soup anytime of the year if you can get fennel with an abundant of green fronds. Unfortunately, the markets have a tendency to cut most them off. -They do not know what they are missing.

Scarola e Fagioli

Escarole and Bean Soup

1-pound dried cranberry beans, cannellini or great northern
2 ounces pancetta, diced
1/2 onion, diced a clove garlic or both
1/3 cup extra-virgin olive oil
5 chopped plum tomatoes. Caned plum tomatoes are fine.
6 cups Escarole, chicory, or any greens of your choice, washed and
chopped
Salt and pepper to taste

Soak the beans overnight in cold water to cover. Drain; place in a pot,
cover with cold water, bring to a boil. Cook for about 1 hours or until tender
Meanwhile, in a pot, cook the pancetta and onion in the olive oil
until golden, about 5 minutes over medium heat. Stir in the tomatoes; cook for another 15 minutes.
Add the beans and escarole into the tomato-pancetta mixture, pour in 4 cups of water and or chicken stock, add salt if necessary. Bring to a boil then simmer for 30 more minutes, stirring frequently. Serve hot. (You can use a 15 ounce can of cannellini beans drained and rinsed but add at the end).

The flavors blend delightfully in this warming soup.

Minestrone may be the most popular Italian soup ever.

When you think of minestrone, you tend to think of a thick soup made with a variety of vegetables. Minestrone can vary from r egion to region depending on the season. Minestrone may range from a thick and dense texture with boiled-down vegetables that may be enriched with pasta or rice, to a more broth-based soup with large quantities of diced and lightly cooked vegetables that may or may not include meats. The best time to make vegetable soup is in the summer when the supply of fresh vegetables are in season. To make great minestrone pay attention to the season and use the specific vegetables each season has to offer, whatever the season, onions, celery, carrots are considered essential to any good minestrone. The addition of meat to flavor the soup is another individual choice add chopped pancetta, or rind of prosciutto (if you can get it), even pieces of sausage to the soup, particularly during the cooler months. Cooked pasta is often added at the end, with extra virgin olive oil and fresh, chopped herbs. Minestrone should be enjoyed year-round. It is a soup is even better if prepared a few days ahead.

Minestrone

Vegetable Soup

2 quarts cups chicken broth, beef or vegetable or you can use
plain water
1/4 cup extra-virgin olive oil
2-ounce minced pancetta (about) (salt pork is a good substitute)
1 medium onion, chopped
2 medium carrots, chopped
2 celery stalks (with leaves) chopped
3 to 4 cloves garlic, chopped
1/2 medium zucchini, chopped
1/4 head Savoy cabbage cored and chopped
7 drained whole, peeled, canned tomatoes, roughly chopped
1/3 cup tubetti, ditilini or other small pasta or broken spaghetti
1 can cannellini beans (about 16 ounces), with or without liquid or
freshly cooked dry beans
1/2 cup finely chopped flat-leaf parsley
1/2 cup freshly grated Parmesan (optional)
Coarse salt and freshly ground black pepper to taste

Heat the oil in a large pot over medium-high heat. Add the pancetta, sauté in oil 1 to 2 minutes add chopped celery and garlic, onions and carrots continue over medium heat (about 10 minutes) or until soft, do not brown, then add the tomatoes (If you have fresh tomatoes use them) stirring occasionally, for 3 minutes. Add the cabbage and cook, uncovered, stirring, until wilted, about 3 minutes more. And then add the broth and bring to a boil. Cook over low heat and Simmer for 30 to 40 minutes.

Stir in the pasta, lower to a simmer, and cook until the pasta is tender, about 10 minutes.

Remove the soup from the heat and stir in the herbs. Add salt and pepper to taste. Serve with a sprinkle of grated cheese and extra-virgin olive oil for drizzling.

Add a Genovese twist. Serve warm, with a drizzle of pesto on top.
You can cook pasta separately, drain then add it at the end.
Cooking the pasta in with the soup will make the soup nice and thick, I like it that way. Adding pasta is not necessary you may like some small cubed potatoes instead.
Soup can be made 2 days ahead and chilled. You may need to add more broth or water to thin.
Omit Tomatoes to make it White or Minestrone Bianco (a nice change)
For fresh beans: Soak beans overnight in cold water. Drain beans, rinse, and place them in a large saucepan or stockpot. Add salt pork or pancetta and 6 cups of broth. Cover and bring to a boil. Reduce heat and cook gently for about 1 hour.

Zuppa di Lenticchie
Lentil Soup

10-ounce bag dried brown lentils (rinsed and drained)
2-3 cloves of garlic chopped
1 onion finely chopped
1-2 stalks of celery chopped fine
1-2 carrots chopped fine
1-2 bay leaves (optional)
Olive oil
2 or 3 plum tomatoes, crushed (optional)
About 6 cups water or chicken broth
Salt and pepper to taste

Sauté garlic, onion, celery, and carrots in the olive oil until translucent stirring 2 to 3 minutes. Add bay leaf and tomatoes if using them.

Add lentils and Add water ore stock to your stock pot to cover the lentils by about 2-3 inches. You can always add more water if it looks too thick.

Turn on high heat till mixture starts to boil and then down to a simmer. Cook for until they start to absorb some of the water. About 20-30 minutes or until the lentils are tender .

Once soup is cooked, adjust your seasonings. Add water to desired consistency,

Lentil soup is one of my favorites. It is easy to make, and delicious. This is a wonderful soup on its own and can be served with bread and salad to make a complete meal. You can add rice or cooked pasta as well as cooked greens, spinach, escarole, or sausage.
In Italy, every region has its own favorite ways of doing things but adding a drizzle of extra virgin olive oil when serving is the best.

Zuppa di Salsicce e Pasta
Sausage and Pasta Soup

2 lbs. sausage hot or sweet
2 carrots, peeled and chopped
1 onion, peeled and chopped
2 stalks celery chopped
2 garlic cloves, peeled and chopped
1- or 2-quarts chicken broth
1 (28 ounce) cans diced tomatoes
3 tbs. olive oil
1 or 2 cans cannellini beans, rinsed and drained
1 or 1 1/2 cups small shell pasta
Escarole or spinach leaves, rinsed and chopped
Salt and freshly ground black pepper

Remove casings from sausages and put them in a stock pot over medium-high heat. Cook them, stirring often and breaking them apart until browned and crumbly, 8 to 10 minutes. Spoon out and discard all but about 1 tablespoon of the fat from pan. Add olive oil. Sauté carrots, onion, celery, and garlic stir often until translucent, about 5 minutes. Add broth, tomatoes with their juice, beans, Bring to a boil. Return sausage and add pasta, reduce heat and simmer, with cover on, stirring occasionally until pasta is cooked, about 10 minutes.
Stir in escarole or spinach and cook just until it is wilted. Add salt and pepper to taste.

Best if made the day before if it gets to thick add water or broth. Parmesan cheese and fresh basil to sprinkle over top to taste.

Pasta e Ceci
Pasta with Chickpeas

2 oz Pancetta chopped
1 small onion, peeled and finely chopped
1 stick of celery, trimmed and finely chopped
Clove of garlic, peeled and finely chopped
Extra virgin olive oil
A sprig of fresh rosemary, leaves picked and finely chopped
1or2 15-oz. cans of chickpeas
2 1/4 cups of chicken stock
1/2 cup chopped tomatoes (optional)
ditalini or other small Italian (I also like broken up pasta)
1/4 cup parmesan cheese
Salt and freshly ground black pepper
Fresh basil or parsley, leaves torn

Put the pancetta, onion, celery, and garlic into a pot with a little extra virgin olive oil and the rosemary. Sauté 5 or 10 minutes until all the vegetables are soft, do not brown.

Drain the chickpeas well and rinse them in cold water and then add them to the pot with the stock. Cook gently for 15 or 20 minutes and then, remove half the chickpeas and put them aside in a bowl.

Puree the soup in the pot using a handheld immersion blender or crush them with a potato masher. Add the reserved whole chickpeas and the pasta, (you can also pre cook the pasta). Season the soup with salt and pepper. Simmer gently until the chickpeas are tender and the pasta is cooked. If the soup is a too thick add broth or water to thin add more salt and pepper if needed. Serve with drizzled extra virgin olive oil, cheese and fresh basil or parsley.

This is both a soup and a pasta dish, but I think it leans slightly more toward being a soup. It is related to pasta e fagioli, I think that this simple, delicious dish, which uses chickpeas as its base, is what Italian food it is all about.

Pasta Fagioli

Pasta and Bean Soup

3 Tablespoons Extra Virgin Olive Oil
pancetta chopped (optional)
1 to 2 garlic cloves chopped and 1medium onion chopped
1 carrot chopped finely
1 stalk of celery chopped finely
1 bay leaf
1 to 2 cans cannellini beans rinsed and drained (if you are using
dried beans soak them overnight and change the water, Cook the
beans in water, until done they should be quite soft)
3 - 4 cups chicken or vegetable broth or water
1 1/2 cup plum tomatoes chopped
Pinch of red Pepper Flakes
1 1/2 cups small tubular short pasta
Grated Romano cheese

In medium size soup pot heat olive oil over medium high heat. Add
pancetta. reduce heat to medium low and cook for 2-3 minutes. Add
in garlic and onions, stir, about 2 minutes. Do not let it burn. Add bay
leaf, carrots, and celery, stir. Reduce heat to simmer and cook for
about 8 minutes. Once carrots and celery are soft add in tomatoes,
beans, water, and broth. Bring to boil then reduce to simmer. Cover
and cook for about 10-20 more minutes. In separate pot bring 6 cups
water to a boil and add pasta. Cook until al dente. Drain and combine
pasta with the soup and stir. Add salt and pepper to taste. Simmer for
another 5 to 10 minutes for flavors to meld. If too thick add broth or
pasta water Serve with Italian grated cheese and a drizzle of extra
virgin olive oil.

*Pasta e fagioli also known as "pasta fazool" a comforting soup that everyone
produced with a different variation. This is one of them. Sometimes I like the
addition of escarole and lots of grated cheese.*

Ribollita
Twice boiled

Soffritto: *A small onion, a small carrot, 2 stalks celery, and a small bunch of parsley, minced together (you can also add 2 ounces of pancetta for extra flavor)*
1-pound dried white beans, washed and soaked for three hours
1/4 cup olive oil
1 1/2 tablespoons tomato paste or 1/2 cup crushed tomatoes (optional)
1/2-pound cavolo nero or black-leaf kale, shredded, (I have used escarole or any dark leaf vegetable, chopped)
1/2-pound beet greens, ribbed and shredded Chicory is a great substitute
1/2-pound potatoes, peeled and diced
Coarse salt and freshly ground pepper
Sprig of thyme (I have used rosemary)
Thinly sliced day-old Italian bread
Olive oil (to be used at the table)
Water or broth if needed (Rebollita should be very thick)

Boil the beans in water until they are almost cooked, sauté the (Soffritto) onion mixture in the oil, in a heavy pot. When the onion has become translucent, add the tomato paste add broth and some liquid from the beans. Add the cabbage, beet greens, and potatoes. Stir in the beans and season to taste with salt, pepper, and a sprig of thyme.
Simmer for 1 hour or until all the vegetables are cooked almost overcooked Add the bread to the soup and simmer for 10 more minutes. Taste for seasoning and serve hot in large bowls sprinkled with Parmesan and drizzled with olive oil.
Rebollita improves dramatically with age, so much that when it is reheated and served the next day.

Ribollita means "twice boiled," referring to the fact that this Tuscan soup was originally simply leftover Minestrone reheated the next day and mixed with chunks of bread. The entire mixture is sometimes baked until bubbly hot, then served with a drizzle of olive oil.

Battuto e Soffritto

The terms Battuto and Soffritto are important to Italian cooking.
Battuto comes from battere, which means "to beat," or in this case, to
mince very fine. Soffritto derives from soffriggere, which means "to
sauté, or fry in a small amount of fat." A Battuto becomes a Soffritto
when it is gently sautéed in fat, usually olive oil. Soffritto is a
mixture of vegetables – usually onion, celery, carrot, garlic, herbs,
and sometimes lardo or pancetta – sautéed in olive oil or butter until
they become soft and caramelized, adding their flavors to any
ingredient that follows. These are usually prepared when making
sauces, stews, and soups.

To make a Battuto, the most effective tool for a Battuto is a
mezzaluna ("rocking knife") chop the vegetables until very fine,
almost the consistency of a paste or food processor, using the pulse
setting.

Sette cose fa la zuppa—
Cava fame e sete attuta,
Empie il ventre e netta il dente,
Fa dormire, fa smaltire,
E fa la quancia arrossire.

*"Soup does seven things. It relieves your hunger, quenches your
thirst, fills your stomach, cleans your teeth, makes you sleep,
helps you digest, and colors your cheeks."*

Secondi Piati

Secondi Piati

Scalopini alla Marsalla

Scalopini di Vitello Piccata

Saltimbocca Alla Romana

Scalopini di Vitello Francese

Cotoletta Alla Milanese

Carne alla Pizzaiola

Pollo e Salsiccia

Pollo con Rosmarino

Pollo sotto Mattone

Pollo Cacciatore

Stracotto di Manzo

Spezzatino di Vitello con Piselli

Ossibuchi alla Milanese

Polpette Semplici

Zucchini Ripiene

Peperoni Ripieni al Forno

Parmigiana di Melanzane al Forno

Melanzana Rollatini

Melanzana Ripieno come Pannini

Salsicce con Cime di Rape

Salsicce e Patate

Salsiccia con Peperoni

Petto d Pollo Impanato

Braciole / Cutina

Vitello Tonato

Scalopini alla Marsalla
Veal Marsala

8 veal cutlets (about 3 ounces each) thinly sliced and pounded
1/4 cup flour
Salt and freshly ground black pepper
2 to 3 tablespoons unsalted butter
2 to 4 tablespoons olive oil
2 to 4 garlic cloves, sliced
2 ounces mushrooms, sliced (optional)
1/2 cup dry Marsala wine
3/4 cup chicken broth
Leaves from 1 fresh rosemary sprig or chopped parsley

Sprinkle the veal with salt and pepper. Dredge in flour.
Melt 1 tablespoon of butter and 1 tablespoon of oil in a heavy large
skillet over medium-high heat. Add 4 veal cutlets and cook until
lightly brown, about 1 1/2 minutes per side. Transfer the veal to a
plate. Repeat with the remaining 4 cutlets. Set the cutlets aside.
Add 1 tablespoon of oil to the skillet. Add the garlic. Sauté, about 30
seconds. Add a tablespoon of the olive oil, if necessary. If using
mushrooms add them and sauté until tender and the juices evaporate,
about 3 minutes. Season with salt. Add the Marsala. Simmer until the
Marsala reduces by half, about 2 minutes. Add the broth and the
rosemary leaves. Simmer until reduced by half, about 4 minutes.
Return the veal to the skillet. Pour in the pan juices. Cook just until
heated through, about 1 or 2 minutes. Stir the remaining 1 tablespoon
of butter into the sauce. Season the sauce with salt and pepper, to
taste. Transfer the veal to plates. Spoon the sauce over the veal and
serve.

Also, excellent to use- chicken or pork cutlets pounded very thin.

Scalopini di Vitello Piccata
Veal Piccata

1 pound thinly sliced veal and pounded
flour for dredging
3 Tablespoons Olive Oil
1/3 cup unsalted butter
2 tablespoons flour
The juice 1 to 2 lemons
1/2 cup   chicken broth or white wine
2 tablespoons capers (optional)
2 tablespoons minced parsley
Salt & pepper

Dredge each piece of veal in flour to coat and shake off excess.
Heat oil in a large sauté pan set on medium heat.
Place veal in pan and cook until lightly browned on both sides, about
2-3 minutes for each side.
Drain the oil and add butter, wine, lemon, salt, and pepper. Cook for
1 minute.
Add the broth and cook until the liquid is reduced by half, 5 to 6
minutes (sprinkle a little flour in when it starts boiling to thicken.)
Transfer Chicken to serving dishes, top with sauce and a slice of
lemon and some capers for garnish.

*Veal Piccata is a Milanese specialty that calls for thinly sliced veal but can   be
made with chicken breasts or pork cutlets pounded very thin.*

Saltimbocca Alla Romana
"Leap in your mouth" Roman Style Veal

4 slices of prosciutto
4 veal scaloppini thinly sliced and pounded
Flour spread on a plate for dredging
2 tablespoons olive oil
2 tablespoons unsalted butter
4 sage leaves
1/2 cup dry white wine
1/4 cup chicken broth
Salt and pepper

Pound the veal in lightly with a meat pounder. Place a thin slice of prosciutto onto each slice of veal and a fresh sage leaf on top of prosciutto. Secure with toothpicks.

Dredge both sides of the scaloppini in flour to coat, shaking off any excess.

Heat olive oil in large sauté pan over medium-high heat. Place the prosciutto side down in the pan and cook, turning once, until lightly browned on both sides. Transfer to a warm plate.

Drain oil from pan, place back over heat and add butter. When butter is melted Add the white wine and scrape loosen any bits from bottom of pan, stirring constantly. When the pan juices are lightly thickened Place scaloppini back in pan, prosciutto side up and cook until sauce is reduced by half and scaloppini are heated through.

Transfer veal to serving plates, spoon sauce over top and serve.

All the scaloppini's are interchangeable with chicken thinly cut and pounded even pork cutlets.

Scalopini Francese
Veal in the French Style

4 veal scaloppini, pounded thin
Salt & pepper
1 egg
3 tbsp. lemon juice
1/4 cup flour
2 tbsp. butter
1 tbsp. vegetable oil
1/3 cup chicken broth or dry white wine

Prepared scaloppini. Season with salt and pepper. In a shallow dish, beat the egg until light with 1 tablespoon of lemon juice. Scatter the flour on a plate.

In a large, skillet, over medium high heat, heat the butter and oil together. When almost hot enough to fry, dip a piece of veal into the flour then into the egg to coat lightly on both sides. Add the coated veal to the skillet and fill up skillet with 1 or 2 more pieces. Sauté quickly on both sides, until batter is lightly browned. Remove to a platter.

Add remaining lemon juice and broth or wine to skillet. Boil vigorously, stirring with a wooden spoon to dissolve any pan browning's and to reduce to a light sauce. Spoon sauce over cooked veal or turn each piece of veal in the sauce before serving at once, drizzled with any extra sauce.

This is a delicious and easy recipe that isn't entirely Italian, you can also have chicken francese, shrimp francese, and fish (usually sole or flounder fillets) francese.
Francese means "in the French manner," it refers to a food that is dipped in flour and egg, fried, then dressed.
I have never had this dish in Italy and it very well may be American Italian, but I feel it fits so well in the scaloppini group.

Cotoletta Alla Milanese

Cutlets Milanese

1-pound veal, chicken, or pork cutlets, pounded thin
2 eggs
Salt and fresh ground pepper to taste
1/2 cup flour
2 cups bread crumbs (optional seasoned- e.g. cheese, parsley salt pepper garlic)
2 vegetable oil
2 tablespoons olive oil

Lightly beat the eggs with the salt in a deep dish and spread the flour and the breadcrumbs out on separate plates. Dredge veal slices in flour shaking off any excess. Then dip in the egg and the bread crumbs, making sure both sides are well coated.
In large sauté pan over medium heat add oil. When the oil is hot add the breaded cutlets to the pan without crowding turning once until golden brown and crispy.

Cotoletta alla Milanese - Milanese Veal Cutlet, is a typical traditional dish from Milan. Served in Italy with the bone in.
It is almost identical to the Wienerschnitzel, a typical traditional dish from Vienna also chicken or pork.

Bistecca alla Pizzaiola
Steak Pizza Style

1 to 1 1/2-pound top round beef or chuck,
28 oz. can tomatoes chopped
1/2 cup water
1/2 cup sliced sweet onions
1 teaspoon dried oregano
Olive oil
Red pepper flakes to taste
salt and pepper to taste

Preheat oven to 350 F.
Heat olive oil in a large skillet and add meat to pan and brown quickly on each side 3-5 minutes.
Remove meat from pan when it is browned and place in baking dish. Add tomatoes, onions and seasonings drizzle some olive on top of steak. Cover with foil and bake for 45 minutes covered. Remove foil and cook an additional 20-30 minutes until tomatoes are cooked down and the meat is tender.

A Neapolitan classic, spicy and delicious and named after the pizza-maker- the sauce is similar.
My mother's way was, a thick slice of chuck or round is used. You can use these cuts if you have time to braise the meat in the oven
for 1 1/2 hours to tenderize these tougher cuts.

Pollo e Salsiccia

Chicken and Sausage

1 4-pound chicken, cut into 10 pieces (sautéed lightly browned)
8 sweet Italian sausages (Sautéed lightly browned)
1 or 2 lemons, halved (more if you like)
4 cloves garlic, peeled and sliced (more if you like)
1/2 cup pure olive oil
Fresh, Rosemary, Parsley, Sage, or dried Bay leaf to taste (or any combination) freshly ground pepper
Coarse salt to tast

Put the chicken and sausage pieces into a dish, squeeze lemon on the chicken add the garlic, olive oil, sage or rosemary, season. Mix well to coat thoroughly. Let the chicken stand at room temperature in the marinade for 30 minutes or overnight refrigerated.

Preheat the oven to 350 F to 375 F.

In a skillet heat a little oil and brown chicken and sausage 15 to 20 minutes. Remove chicken, sausage and the browning's with a little water and add to a large roasting pan with the remaining marinade. Turn the chicken pieces skin side up and season with salt and pepper. Arrange the sausages around the chicken and the fresh Rosemary. Bake for about 1 hour or until the chicken and sausage are nicely browned; turn halfway through cooking add another squeezed lemon at this point if the pan is dry add a little water. Transfer the chicken, sausages, and lemons to a platter, drizzle with some of the pan juices and serve.

The addition of sliced precooked potatoes makes an interesting dish or cook with the chicken and the sausage, (incorporated into the cooking time) or Remove the chicken and sausage from the pan add boiled red potatoes cut up- when potatoes are browned return the chicken and sausage for 5 to 10 minutes.

I use Rosemary, but other times I have use thyme, parsley or Bay leaf and of course extra garlic and lemon. I like it with lots of lemmons. I add one or two lemons extra: it does not matter.

Pollo con Rosmarino
Roast Chicken with Rosemary and Lemon

2 1/2 pounds chicken, cut into pieces
6 cloves garlic, sliced or chopped
3 tablespoons fresh rosemary leaves stripped from stems
3 tablespoons extra-virgin olive oil
1 to 2 lemons, juiced
Coarse salt and fresh ground black pepper
1/2 cup chicken broth

Arrange chicken in a baking dish, 9 by 13-inch. Add garlic, rosemary, extra-virgin olive oil, salt, pepper, and lemon juice to the dish. Toss and coat the chicken with all the ingredients, marinate overnight or for at least 1 hour turning once.
Preheat oven to 375 - 400 F.
Roast 20 minutes. Add chicken broth and more lemon juice if you like and combine with pan juices. Cover with foil and return to oven turn the oven to 350 F and cook for another 30 minutes or until the chicken is tender and almost falls off the bone. Remove chicken from the oven. Place chicken on serving dish, spooning pan juices over the chicken, serve.

My mother would add cooked thin spaghetti to the pan juices (and serve it on the side with the chicken)
Not typical Italian way to serve it but boy was that good!

Pollo sotto Mattone

Chicken under a Brick

1 whole chicken, about 3 pounds trimmed of excess fat, rinsed, dried
and split, backbone removed or cut up chicken
1 tablespoon garlic, coarsely chopped
2 tablespoons extra virgin olive oil
2 sprigs fresh rosemary
1 lemon, cut into quarters
Salt and pepper to taste
Two bricks covered in aluminum foil

Mix together the rosemary leaves, salt, pepper, garlic and 1 tablespoon of the olive oil, and rub this all over the chicken. Cover and marinate in the refrigerator for 30 minutes or overnight. When ready to cook bring chicken to room temperature. Press rosemary sprigs, into the skin side of the chicken. Press down hard to make it as flat as possible.
 Preheat an ovenproof 12-14-inch cast iron skillet or heavy nonstick skillet over medium-high heat for 3 minutes.
Heat olive oil in the pan and wait for it to heat up and just barely begin smoking. Place the chicken in the skillet, skin side down, along with any remaining pieces of rosemary and garlic. Press chicken to flatten in the skillet cover with a piece of aluminum foil. Add the two bricks on the top. The idea is to flatten the chicken by applying weight evenly over its surface.
Cook on stove over medium-high to high heat for 5 minutes to sear then turn heat down (depending on the stove you may have to adjust the heat, try to keep the heat as high as possible) and cook 10 to 15 minutes, turn chicken and return the bricks for another 10 to 15 minutes or until fully cooked. (if you wish you can transfer to the oven. Continue cooking in an oven preheated to 425 F and then roast for 15 minutes more). Serve hot or at room temperature, with lemon wedges.

This is a classic Italian method of cooking chicken resulting in a juicy meat with crispy and highly flavorful crispy skin.

Polo alla Cacciatore
Hunter's Chicken Stew

2 tbsp olive oil
1 whole roasting chicken, cut in pieces
Salt and fresh ground black pepper to taste
1 large onion, sliced
8 oz fresh mushrooms, quartered
4 to 6 cloves garlic, sliced
3 sprigs rosemary
1/2 tsp red pepper flakes, or to taste
1 cup tomato sauce
1/2 cup water or red wine
2 red bell peppers, sliced
Fresh Parsley finely chopped

Season the chicken generously with salt and fresh ground black pepper. Place a heavy Dutch oven, over medium- high heat; add the olive oil and brown the chicken pieces well on all sides. Remove the chicken, and add the onions, mushrooms, and garlic. Reduce the heat to medium and sauté for about 5 minutes, until the onions are translucent.

Add the rosemary, pepper flakes, tomato sauce, and water. Stir to combine. Place the chicken pieces, and any juices in the sauce, and top with the sliced peppers. Cover with the lid and bake in a preheated 350 F oven for 1 hour 15 minutes.

Remove from oven and let rest for 15 minutes. Before serving, taste sauce and adjust seasoning add parsley. Serve .

Cacciatore means "hunter" in Italian, and this classic chicken stew is rustic, easy to make, and delicious. Chicken cacciatore is great served over pasta, rice, or polenta.

Stracotto di Manzo

Italian Pot Roast

3 1/2 to 4-pound rump or chuck beef roast
salt and freshly ground pepper to taste
1/2 cup extra virgin olive oil
1 large carrot, diced
1 large celery stalk, diced
1 medium onion, diced
2 garlic cloves, chopped
2 Tbsp chopped fresh parsley
1 bay leaf
3 cups Italian red wine
1 28-ounce can Italian plum tomatoes, crushed

Season meat with salt and pepper. Heat the oil in a large heavy pot or Dutch oven over medium-high heat. When the oil is hot, add the roast and cook, turning it a few times, until it is nicely browned on all sides, 10-12 minutes. Transfer the meat to a platter. Reduce the heat to medium. Add the carrot, celery, and onion. Cook, stirring occasionally until the vegetables are lightly browned, 10-12 minutes. Add the garlic, parsley, and stir about 1 minute. Add 1 cup of the wine and stir quickly, lifting the browned caramelization that sticks to the bottom of the pan. Return the meat to the pot. Raise the heat, adding the remaining wine, the bay leaf, and the tomatoes, and bring to a boil. Cover the pot, reduce the heat to low, and simmer, turning and basting the meat often, until the meat is very tender and flakes away when pierced with a fork, 3-4 hours. Turn off the heat and let the roast sit in its juices for 10 minutes. Remove the meat from the pot and cover loosely with foil. If the sauce is too thin, cook more and reduce it until it has a medium-thick consistency. Taste and adjust seasoning. Slice meat and serve with gravy.

Can be made as a stew just add more vegetables and use stew meat instead of a roast. Delicious over Italian rice (Aborio).

Spezzatino di Vitello con Piselli
Veal Stew with Peas

1 1/2-pounds lean stewing veal
1 cup fresh peas or frozen peas
1/3 cup olive oil
2 ribs celery, finely diced
1 small onion, chopped
1 medium carrot, finely diced
1 tablespoon finely chopped parsley
6 tablespoons tomato chopped
1 cup veal or chicken broth or good dry white wine, or both
Coarse salt and freshly ground pepper to taste

Cut the meat into 1 1/2-inch cubes.
Shell or defrost the peas
Heat the olive oil in a pot then add the veal and turn it until lightly browned. Then add the celery, onion, carrot, and parsley. Cook, stirring often or until the onion becomes translucent, about 5 minutes.
Add tomato sauce, broth, or wine, and some salt and pepper. Reduce the heat to very low and simmer gently. Cook uncovered, being careful that the sauce does not stick. If it becomes too thick add a little water, broth, or wine. Simmer the stew for a full hour and a half, The meat should be very tender when tested with a fork, but it should not be completely falling apart. Add the peas cook for an additional 10 minutes At the end of cooking time the sauce should be thick and rich .Serve with polenta or rice.

Ossibuchi alla Milanese
Veal Shanks Milanese Style

4 veal shanks an inch thick and 6-7 inches across,
about 2 pounds *
Flour
1 small onion, diced
1 small carrot, diced
1 stalk celery, diced
2 tablespoons olive oil
Salt and pepper to taste
1/2 cup dry white wine
2/3 cup hot broth or water more if needed
1-2 tablespoons tomato sauce or 2 teaspoons tomato paste
diluted in water

Gremolada *(a mixture of herbs added at the end)*
2 cloves garlic
Fresh leaves of a 6-inch sprig of rosemary
A small bunch of parsley
The zest of a small lemon, grated
1-2 anchovies, rinsed and boned (quite optional)

(I prefer to make a Gremolada with finely chopped lemon zest and parsley and sprinkled on the top before serving)

Make cuts at several points in the membranes surrounding the shank or they will shrink and causing them to curl as they cook. (This is important) Put the oil in a heavy bottomed pan or Dutch oven large enough to hold the veal shanks without stacking them. Meanwhile, season with salt and pepper then flour the veal shanks and brown on both sides, when brown remove, and reserve, then add butter sauté the onion carrot and celery sprinkling them every now and then with the wine.

When the wine is completely evaporated, return the veal shanks
to the pot, and add the broth and tomato paste. Check the seasoning and
simmer, covered, until done (about two hours - the meat should be very
tender). If need be, add more broth to keep the veal shanks
from drying out. While the ossibuchi are simmering, prepare the
gremolada by mincing and combining the ingredients. When the veal
shanks are done, remove them to a platter. Reduce the sauce, if necessary .
Cook the sauce for another minute,
And then pour it over the meat and serve, over a bed of plain Aborio rice
or Risotto alla Milanese. Purists also prefer that their Ossibuchi be served
on a bed of plain white rice - Italian risotto rice such as Arborio however,
many people prefer to serve Ossibuchi on a bed of risotto alla milanese, a
tasty saffron-laced risotto.

*The dish is expensive to make and due to the high cost of the veal I
suggest you go to a good butcher and have the shanks cut to the proper
size for Ossibuchi*

Polpette

Meatballs are true home cooking, you are unlikely to find any in a restaurant, but maybe in most homestyle type of trattorias, that cater to local clientele. Nor are you likely to have been served them if you are invited to someone's house, unless you are considered family. Spaghetti and meatballs, this dish is virtually nonexistent in Italy- though a variation of polpette in tomato sauce is found in southern Italy, it is served as a main course and not with pasta. top with a tomato sauce if you like, with a salad or vegetable on the side.

Polpette Semplici
Simple Meatballs

1 pound not-too-lean ground beef
1 cup day-old Italian bread
Water
A large egg
1/4 cup minced parsley or Fresh Basil
A good amount of Grating Cheese
Chopped Garlic or onion or both to taste
Salt & pepper to taste
Vegetable oil for frying

Soak the bread in enough water so it is thoroughly moist. Drain it well; squeezing it gently to remove most of the water, you want the bread moist but not dripping. Combine the bread with the ground meat, egg, the minced parsley, salt, and pepper to taste, and knead the mixture well. Should the meatballs come out to soft, work some finely ground breadcrumbs into them to thicken them.
Then shape it into balls about two in diameter or what you prefer.
Set a large skillet to heat with the oil and add the meatballs. Cook over medium high heat until they are browned on all sides,

To add even more moisture to the meatballs. add more bread, and in the summer lots of fresh Basel.

Polpettone
Meat Loaf

Polpettone is made with a meatball mixture shaped and formed like a meatloaf and baked. Perfect for a cold winter evening!

Zucchini Ripiene
Zucchini with Stuffing

6 zucchinis of the same size
1/4-pound ground beef
Italian sausage, peeled and crumbled
day-old bread, crusts removed and crumbled
Grated Parmigiano
1 egg
1 clove garlic
A medium-sized onion
Small bunch fresh parsley
1 tablespoon unsalted butter
2 tablespoon olive oil
Fresh Parsley
Tomato sauce
Salt & pepper to taste
Grated Mozzarella

Moisten the bread in water. Cut the zucchini in half and scoop out the pulp. Mince the pulp with the onion, garlic, and parsley, and sauté the mixture in the oil until it is lightly browned and transfer to a bowl. Squeeze the bread dry and combine, the egg, the cheese, and the meats with the vegetable mixture. Mix well and season the stuffing to taste with salt, pepper, Basil or Parsley.

Preheat your oven to 350F. Fill the zucchini with the stuffing, pressing it down firmly. Arrange the zucchini in an oiled pan, cover them with the tomato sauce, drizzle with olive oil, and bake them for 30 to 40 minutes, basting regularly with the pan drippings. Add grated Mozzarella and extra cheese. Return to oven for 10 minutes and until cheese is melted .

Stuffed zucchinis are a great second dish, and these, have a meat filling, also can be a meatless dish with the use of rice or bread instead of meat will also work. They will be good both hot and room temperature.

Peperoni Ripieni al Forno
Baked Stuffed Peppers

4 bell peppers
1/2 cup rice preferably Arborio
1/3-pound ground beef or Pork
4 garlic cloves chopped
1/2 cup fresh chopped parsley or basil
Salt and pepper to taste
1 egg
3 Tablespoons extra virgin olive oil
1 1/2 cup tomato sauce
Grated Italian cheese to taste

Preheat oven to 350 F.

Heat olive oil over medium heat in a frying pan. Add garlic and sauté for about 1-2 minutes. Add meat and cook until lightly browned .

Cook the rice in a sauce pan set aside.

When meat is fully cooked, add rice, egg, salt and pepper the parsley or basil and grated cheese - at this point you can add 2-3 tablespoons of sauce to moisten. Mix well.

Cut tops off of peppers and remove seeds and save to use as covers.

Stuff the peppers with mixture and place lids on top.

Place in pre-greased baking dish and place in oven.

Spoon on tomato sauce, drizzle with olive oil, cook until pepers are soft. 25 - 40 minutes depending on the type and size of peppers used. Serve warm.

For some added taste and texture some cubed mozzarella added to the filling.

Parmigiana di Melanzane al Forno
Baked Eggplant with Tomatoes and Mozzarella

2 large eggplants
Oil for cooking
1 garlic clove, finely chopped
1 28 oz can tomatoes, preferably plum, peeled and chopped
Mozzarella cheese
Parmesan cheese, grated
fresh basil leaves
Coarse salt and freshly ground black pepper

Cut the eggplants into slices. Sprinkle with salt and leave in a colander to draw out the excess water. Rinse and pat dry with paper towels. Heat enough oil in a frying pan over medium-high heat and add the eggplant slices in a single layer. Fry on both sides for a few minutes until the slices start to brown slightly. Make sure that the oil is hot before adding the eggplants to the pan So that they do not absorb too much oil. Remove from the pan with a slotted spoon and drain on paper towels. Meanwhile, preheat the oven to 350F. Make a tomato sauce by heating a little oil in a saucepan over medium heat. Add the garlic and cook until soft and transparent, add the tomatoes and basil. Season with salt and black pepper. Cook for 10 minutes until the tomatoes have broken up and reduced into a sauce. When the sauce is ready, arrange alternate layers of eggplant, tomato sauce, slices of mozzarella, and Parmesan in a greased baking dish. Make sure that you press down the ingredients well, so that you end up with compacted layers. Finish off with a layer of sauce and a sprinkling of Parmesan. Bake in the preheated oven for about 40 minutes. Let stand for a few minutes to allow the ingredients to set. and then cut into individual portions. slide out onto serving plates using a spatula and serve hot.
Another method is to lightly batter (page 183) the eggplant before you fry them and then continue with the recipe.

Rollatini di Melanzane
Rolled Eggplant

2/3 cup vegetable oil
1 medium eggplant cut lengthwise into 1/4-inch·thick slices
2 eggs, beaten with 2 tablespoons water
1 1/4 cups dried breadcrumbs (You can use seasoned)

Filling
1 cup ricotta cheese
1 cup grated mozzarella cheese
Grated Italian cheese to taste
Chopped parsley or basil to taste
Salt and pepper to taste
4 cups simple Tomato Sauce
Additional grated mozzarella cheese

Heat oil in a large skillet at medium high heat.
Dip one eggplant slice into eggs. Dip into breadcrumbs, coating
completely. Add to skillet and cook until browned, about 3 minutes
per side. Drain on paper towels. Repeat with remaining eggplant.
Preheat oven to 350 F.
Add some ricotta over each eggplant slice. Sprinkle with mozzarella
. Roll up jelly roll fashion, starting at one short end. Spread 2 cups
tomato sauce in bottom of 9 x13-inch baking dish. Place rolls on
sauce seam side down. Pour remaining 2 cups sauce over eggplant
rolls Sprinkle with additional mozzarella and grated cheese. Bake
until cheese is melted and lightly browned, about 30 minutes.

I think this is American Italian with Italian roots, but I am not sure.

Melanzana Ripieno come Pannini
Eggplant Sandwiches

1 large eggplant
Vegetable oil for frying
8 ounces mozzarella, sliced
Sauce
1 tablespoon extra-virgin olive oil
1 small onion or clove garlic or both
1 28 ounce can tomatoes, chopped
Salt and freshly ground pepper

Filling I
2 cups grated bread crumbs
1/2 cup freshly grated Parmigiano
1 egg
1 clove garlic minced
Fresh parsley or Basil
Salt and freshly ground pepper
1 tablespoon extra-virgin olive oil
Water (enough to make a soft stuffing)
or
Filling II
8 ounces chopped meat
1/2 cup freshly grated cheese
1small onion or garlic clove minced
1 egg
Fresh parsley or Basil
Bread crumbs or stale bread soaked in water
Salt and freshly ground pepper
(Should be like a meatball mixture)

Slice the eggplant into 1/2-inch-thick rounds. Assemble the sandwiches take two eggplant rounds. Distribute mixture 1/2 inch thick and place another slice on top. Like a sandwich.

In a skillet add olive oil and over medium high heat Place each of sandwiches in skillet brown lightly on one side and carefully turning with a spatula and brown the other side, when lightly browned remove sandwiches and reserve. In the skillet heat some olive oil, add garlic, onion or both, sauté -do not brown, add tomatoes salt and pepper and cook over medium heat to create a sauce, cook for 15 minutes then return the eggplant sandwiches to the sauce and continue cooking covered and on a low heat cook until both eggplant and filling are cooked. Add the mozzarella on the top. Place in the oven broiler until the mozzarella melts, about 4 minutes.

I also cook these in the oven about 350 F. Sauté the eggplant sandwiches then put them in a baking dish make the sauce. When the sauce is done, I put it over the eggplant, cover and cook for about 20 to 30 minutes then uncover an add mozzarella and cheese, return for another 10 to 15 minutes .

Salsicce con Cime di Rape

Sausage with Broccoli Rabe

1 tablespoon olive oil
8 links Italian sausages
broccoli rabe, trimmed (boil until tender and drained)
1/4 cup extra-virgin olive oil
1 garlic clove, minced
Red pepper flakes to taste
Salt to taste

Add the sausages to the pan with a little oil. Cook over low heat for 20 minutes, or until browned on both sides. Remove the sausages from the pan and keep them warm. Add olive oil, garlic, chili, Sauté do not brown, then add the cooked broccoli rabe to the pan. Cover the pan and cook for 15 minutes. Return the sausages to the pan for 5 minutes and the dish is ready.

Salsicce e Patate

Sausage and Potatoes

8 links sausages
2 ounces or pancetta chopped (optional)
2 large potatoes or 4 small
2 large cloves garlic
2 tablespoons extra virgin olive oil
Salt and pepper to taste
Warm water or broth
Lemon juice to taste

Peel and slice or dice the potatoes place in cold water.
Cook the sausage links until brown. Remove sausage from skillet .
Slice or mince the garlic and the pancetta. Add oil, heat then add the potatoes and other minced ingredients; cook, stirring, until the garlic begins to brown, add lemon juice some water or broth if needed and simmer until the potatoes are done.

Return sausage to the skillet and add more lemon if desired adjust salt and pepper. Simmer until all the flavors meld together 10 to 15 minutes.

Sausage and potatoes one of the greatest combinations served with a side dish of sautéed broccoli rabe. What could be better? A glass of Chianti -maybe.

Salsiccia con Peperoni
Sausage and Peppers

2 - 3 Peppers, seeds removed. cut in strips
8 links sausage (cut in bite size bits)
Olive oil
Onion (cut in big strips or chunks)
2 cloves garlic sliced or minced
Salt pepper to taste

Fry sausage pieces in a large skillet until browned and cooked. Add oil, onion and garlic, peppers, fry everything together until brown. Adjust seasoning. Better when it is slightly over cooked.

Peppers, eggs, and sausage; Cut up sausage, return everything to skillet add 4 beaten eggs scramble add some grated cheese and you have Peppers and Eggs.

Use this recipe as a guide for other ingredients such as zucchini and eggs, asparagus, and eggs and just potatoes and eggs. Delicious! Great in a sandwich.

Petto d Pollo Impanato

Breaded Chicken Breasts

Vinegar
Garlic
Oil
Chicken cutlets
Bread crumbs (Seasoned or plain)
Italian Parsley, chopped
Grated Italian cheese
Extra virgin olive oil.
Baking pan
Salt and freshly ground pepper

Marinate chicken in oil, vinegar, garlic salt and pepper. At least 1/2 hour or more.

Preheat oven to 375 F.

Drizzle some olive oil on bottom of pan and spread to cover pan. Set aside. Add bread crumbs, parsley, cheese, salt and pepper in a bowl and mix together. Dip chicken breasts in mixture and coat both sides. Place breaded chicken breast in pan do not overlap. Add more oil if needed to the pan.

Bake for 35 minutes. turn and Bake for another 10 - 15 minutes to allow mixture to get crispy. Remove and serve. Be careful not to overcook otherwise the chicken will dry out.

My mother made this dish quite often, be careful not to dry them out. A good alternative to frying .

Braciole

Beef Roll

3 tablespoons olive oil
Beef round braciole
1/2 cup bread crumbs (seasoned if you like)
1/2 cup grated parmesan cheese
3 garlic cloves or onion or both, (chopped)
1/2 cup fresh parsley or Basil, chopped
Salt and pepper to taste
1 cup dry red wine (Optional)
Imported Italian tomatoes
1/4 cup fresh basil leaves, torn into pieces

Pound each piece of the beef into thin slices about 1/4 inch thick. Mix garlic, parsley or basil, cheese, and bread crumbs in a bowl. Lay round steak flat. Spread mixture of bread crumbs, minced garlic, onion, chopped parsley and grated cheese over each beef slice, salt, and pepper them and roll up into a small bundle, securing each with toothpicks.

Heat the oil in a large skillet and brown the beef well on all sides, about 3-4 minutes. Remove the braciole from the pot, Transfer to a separate dish, Add the wine, and cook up until it is reduced by half, scraping up the browned bits from the bottom of the skillet. Add the tomatoes, and season with salt and pepper. Return the braciole to the pot and Cook over medium heat, until the sauce has begun to thicken, simmer for 45 minutes. Cook until tender and sauce is reduced. Serve hot with a side dish of your choice. This method of cooking the braciole also produces a rich tomato sauce, which can be served with pasta of your choice.

Tender beef rolls cooked in a robust tomato and wine sauce. They go perfectly with a side dish of Risotto Milanese or polenta.

Cotenne / Cutina
Sicilian Pork Skin Roll

2-3 pork skins for Cutina (purchase at an Italian pork store)
1 cup flavored bread crumbs page (227)
2 garlic cloves, chopped
1/4 cup onion chopped
parsley
Grated Italian cheese
Tomato Sauce
Salt and pepper to taste
1/4 cup olive oil to drizzle

Clean off the slabs of pigskin Lay skin flat, shiny side down.
Sprinkle breadcrumbs then sprinkle all other dry ingredients on the skin.
Once all ingredients are on skin, drizzle with olive oil Roll skins tightly.
Tie with cooking twine in several places so they do not come apart
while cooking. Cook in your favorite tomato sauce until tender,
a minimum of 1 to 1 1/2 hour, preferably the duration of the sauce
cooking time.

This is a Sicilian delicacy. I remember my grandmother cooking it for hours in the sauce until it was very tender and melted in your mouth.

Vitello Tonnato

Veal with Tuna Sauce

2 pounds boneless veal, turkey breast or pork, seasoned with salt
pepper and roasted and cooled

Tuna Sauce

1 7-oz. can imported Italian tuna, packed in olive oil (no substitute)

4 flat anchovy filets

1/2 cup extra-virgin olive oil

3 tsp. lemon juice, freshly squeezed

3 tbsp. capers, soaked and rinsed

3/4 cup mayonnaise

Garnishes: *your choice- Thin slices of lemon, slivered, Oil cured black olives, whole capers, Italian parsley leaves.*

Drain tuna and put into a food processor with anchovies, olive oil, lemon juice, and capers. Process until it becomes a creamy, beige-colored sauce. Fold sauce gently, but thoroughly, into the mayonnaise. Or combine all the sauce ingredients in a food processor. Blend until smooth.

When meat has cooled, transfer to a cutting board. Carefully cut into thin slices.

Spread some of the tuna sauce on bottom of a platter. Place a single layer of veal slices; cover with sauce. Repeat layering, ending a good amount of sauce.

Cover veal with plastic wrap and refrigerate for at least 24 hours. Bring to room temperature before serving. garnish with some or all of the suggested garnishes.

This dish is so refreshing in the summer it may take you a few bites to acquire a taste for it but when you do your hooked.

A classic summer dish in northern Italy is Vitello Tonnato, or veal blanketed in a rich tuna sauce. But the traditional dish requires a boneless veal roast which is not only difficult to find in the US but can also be quite expensive. This recipe is a simplified version of the classic dish. You can substitute a roasted pork loin or a boneless turkey breast .

Pesce

Secondo Piati

Pesce

Pesce alla Griglia
Pesce Spada alla Siciliana
Fritto Misto di Mare
Calamari Fritto
Pesce alla Francese
Baccalà I II
Insalata di Frutti di Mare
Gamberetti con Aglio e Burro
Zuppa Di Pesce
Vongole Posillipo
Zuppa di Vongole e Cozze
Spaghetti allo Scoglio
Spaghetti con Vongole
Risotto a Frutta di Mare

Pesce alla Griglia

Grilling Fish

Fish steaks or whole fish (any small fish e.g. sea bass, orata,
branzino, salmon, tuna, swordfish, haddock, or fresh cod)
1/2 cup olive oil
1 lemon
1 garlic clove
5 sprigs fresh rosemary
2 Tablespoons fresh parsley, chopped
Coarse salt and fresh ground black pepper

Chop the garlic, rosemary, parsley, salt, and pepper until everything
is mixed add the olive oil and the juice the lemon in a small bowl.
Brush both sides of the fish with the mixture, place the fish, on a hot
grill (or under a broiler or in a skillet).
When the first side is browned, turn over carefully.
Brush with the oil-lemon mixture and cook until both sides are
browned, and the fish begins to flake.
Italians love to grill seafood. Grilling can bring out the delicate
flavors of fish. Start with thick steaks rather than thin fillets. Tuna,
swordfish, or salmon steaks should be 1 1/2-inch-thick for the best
results. Or a whole fish e.g. Sea Bass.
Begin with good fresh fish and you will not need to over season it to
give it flavor just brush the fish with a little olive oil and lemon juice
before cooking or mince fresh herbs and sprinkle them around the
fish with a little coarse salt.

Served with a bread salad and a side of grilled vegetables and a glass of
chilled white wine is a perfect summer dish. What could be better?

Pesce Spada alla Siciliana
Grilled Sicilian Swordfish

Extra-virgin olive oil, plus extra
Swordfish steaks, about 6 ounces each
Salt and freshly ground pepper
Capers packed in brine
Chopped parsley
Juice of 1 lemon, plus extra

In a large skillet over medium heat, warm 4 tablespoons of olive oil.
Season the swordfish steaks with salt and pepper and add to the
skillet. Cook for about 4 minutes on each side. Transfer to plates and
keep warm.
Drain and coarsely chop the capers. Add to the skillet along with the
parsley. Stir with a wooden spoon to remove any browned bits from
the bottom of the skillet. Remove from the heat, deglaze with the
lemon juice, and stir.
Place the swordfish steaks on each of 4 plates and distribute the
lemon-caper sauce over. To serve, drizzle the swordfish with more
lemon juice and olive oil.

*Sicilians know how to catch fish, how to prepare fish, how to cook fish, and
how to eat fish.*

Fritto Misto di Mare
Mixed Fried Seafood

Calamari (squid, cut into rings) with tentacles
Large shrimp, cleaned and deveined
Firm white fish (like halibut, sea bass, cod, and
if you can get smelts or small fresh sardines etc.)
Enough oil for frying at 375 F
Enough flour to dust (1/2 flour 1/2 semolina)
Coarse salt and pepper to taste
lemons cut into wedges

Clean, wash, and dry the fish well. Small fish are usually cleaned
and just floured.

Thoroughly clean squid and out and cut into rings. Cut fish into bite-
sized pieces. Dust squid, shrimp, and fish with flour. Before you put
them in the oil give them a good shake to dislodge excess flour,
Heat oil (375 F) in a large pan or use a deep fryer. Add seafood in
thirds. Fry until surface is crispy. Remove with a slotted spoon and
let drain on paper towels. Salt them after they are fried, while they
are still hot.

To serve: Add seafood to serving platter. Drizzle with lemon juice
and serve with added lemon wedges. Season with salt and pepper.

*In Italy, Frito Misto di Mare is usually served as a first or second plate. It is
also great as an appetizer on the table for all to share with lots of lemon
wedges and lots of white wine.*

Calamari Fritto
Fried Calamari

Oil, for deep frying
1-pound clean squid with tentacles, bodies cut into 1/3 to 1/2-inch-
thick rings
1/2 all-purpose flour
1/2 semolina flour
Coarse salt and freshly ground black pepper
2 lemons cut into wedges

Pour enough oil into a heavy large saucepan to reach the depth of 3
inches or use a deep fryer.
Fry at medium heat to 375 degrees.
In a medium bowl, combine flours, salt, and pepper.
In small batches, dredge the squid in the flour mixture to coat.
Carefully add the squid to the oil and fry until crisp and golden
brown, about 1 minute per batch (do not overcrowd).
Using a slotted spoon, drain on wire rack or paper towels.
Serve with lemon wedges.

Keep it simple. It should not mask the taste of the squid.
There are a lot of recipes for calamari fritto but here is a simple one. Makes a
wonderful antipasto or main dish. Be careful not to overcook the calamari. It
will get tough.
I love fried calamari!

Pesce alla Francese
Classic Meunière

Flounder, sole or any other white fish filet
2 to 4 fillets (each about 3 to 4 ounces)
1/2 cup all-purpose flour
Coarse kosher salt
Freshly ground black pepper
2 tablespoons vegetable oil or canola oil
2 tablespoons unsalted butter

Sauce
1/4 cup (1/2 stick) unsalted butter, cut into 4 pieces
2 tablespoons chopped fresh Italian parsley
1-2 tablespoon fresh lemon juice or to taste
Lemon wedges

Place flour in a dish. Rinse fish and pat with paper towels. Sprinkle both sides of fish with coarse salt and freshly ground pepper. Dredge fish on both sides with flour; shake off excess.
Heat oil in large skillet over medium-high heat until oil is hot and shimmers. Add butter; quickly swirl skillet to coat add fish and cook until golden on bottom, 2 to 3 minutes. Carefully turn fish over and cook until opaque in the center and golden on bottom, 1 to 2 minutes. Divide fish between plates; cover with foil.
Pour off drippings from skillet.
Place skillet over medium-high heat. Add butter; cook until golden, 1 to 2 minutes. Remove from heat; stir in parsley and lemon juice. Spoon sauce over fish. Serve with lemon wedges. serves 2 to 4

Meunière is of French, not Italian origin, but it became extremely popular in Italian-American restaurants-probably because of the simplicity of its preparation and the availability of different kinds of fish.

Baccalà

All baccalà requires soaking before it can be used since it is salted. Italian specialty markets sell baccalà it comes 1/2 to 1-inch thick, in 3 to 6-inches and about 12 to 18 inches long and are white on the flesh side. To prepare it, rinse the salt off it and soak it in cold water for 12 or more hours or up to three days depending upon its thickness (refrigerate it in hot weather), changing the water 2-3 times daily. Once it has soaked it is ready for use.

Baccala con Olive
Bacala Stew with Olives

1/4 cup olive oil
3 garlic cloves, thinly sliced
1/2 cup diced onion
1/2 teaspoon red pepper flakes or to taste
6 (8-oz.) salt cod pieces pre -soaked)
1 28 oz. can whole peeled tomatoes with juice
1/2 - 1 cup diced celery
10 to 12 oil cured dried black Sicilian olives with pits
2 cups diced red cooked potatoes (if you do not use the potatoes you
can serve the baccala over pasta)
Salt and pepper to taste

In a large skillet, combine olive oil, garlic, onion, celery, and Red pepper flakes. Cook on medium high for 3 minutes. Add the tomatoes and crush with a spoon, salt to taste. Bring to a boil, reduce to a simmer then cook 10 to 20 minutes, Add the cod and black olives cook 2 to 3 minutes until the cod flakes. Let rest until the flavors meld (add potatoes if you are adding them) then remove from heat. Serve with crusty bread.

Traditionally at our house this baccala stew was served without the potatoes but instead over pasta on Christmas Eve. A second dish would be fried fish and then hopefully some fried savory zeppole. In the center would be a bit of anchovy. On the first bite into that soft breadlike dough it would give way to the saltiness of the anchovies.
That was heaven. That was Christmas Eve.

Baccala Indorato e Fritto
Fried Baccala

2 pounds salted dried cod soaked (Baccala)
2 egg plus enough water to make an egg wash
Flour, seasoned with salt and pepper or 1/2 flour and 1/2 seasoned
bread crumbs
1/2 cup Oil for frying

Put cod in a large bowl and cover with cold water. Soak cod, changing water 3 times a day, up to 3 days or more and then remove the skin and as many of the bones as you can. Drain and chill until ready to use. Pat dry and cut into smaller pieces. Dip in egg wash and Dredge cod with flour.
Heat olive oil in skillet over medium-high heat.
Add the cod and pan fry, 2 minutes on each side until lightly browned
Drain on paper towel serve hot or made into a salad served at room temperature, if you like.

To make a salad
Fried Baccala cut into small pieces
Fresh chopped garlic
Vinegar
Salt and pepper
Oregano
Fresh parsley
Chopped celery
Drizzle with olive oil as you would a salad
Also made with fresh Cod but Traditionally salt cod

Fond memories of Christmas for many Italians, Fried Baccala or Baccala Indorato e Fritto: an important part of the Christmas Eve dinner.

Insalata di Mare
Seafood Salad

1/4-pound calamari tubes, cut into 1/2-inch rings
1/2-pound large shrimp, peeled and deveined
1/2-pound bay scallops
Scungilli (optional) 1 small can
2-3 stalks celery, sliced
1 Diced red or green pepper or both
Flat-leaf parsley, chopped
Red pepper flakes (a generous pinch or more)
Black oil cured olives
Salt to taste

Dressing
1/4 cup fresh lemon juice
1/4 cup extra-virgin olive oil
1 to 2 cloves garlic chopped, or 1 small red onion sliced (I prefer the garlic)
2 Anchovies crushed (optional)

Bring a large pot of water to a boil. Add the calamari and cook until tender 2-4 minutes. Remove from water with a slotted spoon, rinse under cold water to cool then place them in a large bowl. Add the shrimp to the boiling water and cook until pink 3-5 minutes. Drain and run under cold water to cool and add them to the bowl with the calamari. Drain scungilli and add to the bowl. Then the the celery, garlic, parsley, lemon juice and olive oil to the bowl and toss well add salt if needed. Toss until mixed well. Let rest for an hour or two or overnight in the refrigerator Transfer to a serving platter or individual plates and serve.

I like to keep the choice of seafood simple for this cold seafood salad, but if you wanted to add more varieties you could. This makes a great antipasto for a traditional all Fish Italian Christmas Eve dinner.
It can be part of antipasti as first plate on a warm summer night.

Gamberetti con Aglio e Burro
Shrimp with Garlic Sauce

1 to 1 1/2-pound Large shrimp, shelled and deveined tails on
3 tablespoons olive oil (more if needed)
3 tablespoons unsalted butter
4 to 5 cloves garlic, thinly sliced
1 pinch dried red pepper flakes or to taste
1/2 cup dry white wine (optional)
Salt and pepper to taste
Fresh italian Parsley, chopped

Clean and pat shrimp dry.
In a large skillet, heat half of the butter and half of olive oil on high until just starting to smoke. Add 1/2 of the garlic then the shrimp, cook about 3 minutes. Add the wine if you are using and turn shrimp over. Cook 1 to 2 minutes. Add salt, pepper and parsley.
Let the shrimp sauté in the pan over high heat for 2-3 minutes, then turn them and add the rest of the garlic butter and oil parsley and the red pepper. Wait one minute and then mix well and turn off the heat. Remove and serve with crusty bread. Pour the sauce over the shrimp, season with salt and pepper to taste and toss to combine. Serve with sliced lemon.

Zuppa Di Pesce
Fish Soup

1 lb. cleaned squid, bodies and tentacles separated but kept intact
1/2 lb. large shrimp peeled and deveined leaving tail intact
1/4 cup olive oil
3 garlic cloves, finely chopped
1/2 teaspoon red pepper flakes
1/4 teaspoon dried oregano, (optional)
1/2 cup dry white wine (Optional)
12 small hard-shelled clams such as littlenecks, scrubbed
12 mussels scrubbed and beards removed
1 cup fish stock or bottled clam juice
1 (28-oz) can plum tomatoes diced with juice
Coarse salt to taste
1/4 cup chopped fresh flat-leaf parsley
Extra-virgin olive oil for drizzling

Rinse squid and other fish under cold running water and pat dry. Cut the tentacles in half. Cut bodies crosswise into 1/4-inch-thick rings. Clean and devein shrimp and pat dry.

Heat some oil in a wide 6- to 8-quart heavy pot over moderately high heat until hot, then sear shrimp turning over once, until golden but not cooked through, about 2 minutes per batch. Transfer shrimp with a slotted spoon to a bowl.

Add olive oil, garlic, red pepper flakes, and oregano to pot and sauté, stirring, until golden not brown, about 30 seconds. Add tomatoes, wine (if you are using it) and fish stock and bring to a boil. Stir in clams and mussels, shrimp squid and other fish and cook, covered, over moderately high heat until shells open wide, discard any clams or muscles that do not open , checking frequently after 6 minutes and simmer, uncovered, then remove from heat and let stand, covered 1 minute. Stir in parsley and serve drizzled with olive oil.

Vongola Posillipo
Clams Posillipo

3 dozen littleneck clams, scrubbed
1/4 cup olive oil
3 large garlic cloves, minced
1/2 cup canned tomatoes crushed with added puree
1/2 cup fish stock or bottled clam juice
1 teaspoon dried oregano, crumbled
Minced fresh parsley

Heat oil in heavy large skillet over medium heat. Add garlic and sauté 1 minute. Add crushed tomatoes, fish stock and oregano and bring to boil. Add clams, cover, and cook until clams open, about 7 minutes. Discard any clams that do not open. Divide clams and sauce among bowls. Sprinkle with parsley.

This dish is named after a town southwest of Naples that is known for its seafood.
Posillipo is probably Naples's most beautiful and exclusive quarter, where the folk song, "A Marechiaro", was written.

Zuppa di Vongole e Cozze
Clam and Mussel Soup

Small clams, and mussels
cup olive oil
3 cloves garlic
Freshly chopped parsley
Red pepper flakes

Purge the shellfish by soaking them in salted water
In a large pot and sauté the garlic in the oil until it is golden but not browned, then drain the soaking shellfish and add to the pot. Add pepper to taste and cook over a brisk flame, shaking the pot, until all the shellfish have opened. Serve on a large platter that will hold all the juices, add parsley, and serve.
Note: For a red sauce add 1/2 to 1 cup of chopped San Marzano tomatoes sauté with garlic and oil for 5 minutes.

This is classic, simple Neapolitan fare.(I like this dish very garlicky and a bit spicy)

Spaghetti allo Scoglio
Reef Spaghetti

What goes into this dish it depends upon what is available but, here
is a suggestions.

1 1/4 pounds fresh live clams

1 1/4 pounds fresh mussels

12 ounces shelled shrimp tails on

3 to 4 plum tomato (optional)

Fresh parsley or basil roughly chopped

2 to 4 cloves garlic

Extra virgin Olive Oil

Red pepper flakes

Salt if needed

3/4 to 1-pound thin spaghetti or linguini fini

Scrub the shells of the clams and mussels. Shell the shrimp but leave
the tails. Salt a pot of water for the spaghetti and set it to boil. Heat
olive oil in a large skillet. Add garlic and red pepper. Stir until lightly
browned. Stir in tomatoes (if using them) and simmer 5 minutes.
Break up tomatoes. Add seafood. Cover and simmer about 4 minutes
until clams and mussels open. Do not try to open any that did not
open when heated. Discard them.

While the sauce is simmering, cook the spaghetti. Transfer the
cooked spaghetti into a bowl, add the fish and a turn of olive oil,
parsley, and toss. Stir in the sauce and serve.

I added lobster one Christmas Eve and it was spectacular.
Reef spaghetti, or Spaghetti alla Scoglio, is made with all sorts of crustaceans
and shellfish, and is very popular, especially at festive occasions.

Spaghetti con Vongole
Spaghetti with Clams

1-pound linguini fini or a spaghetti
Fresh littleneck clams (You may substitute canned clams) or add a
small can of chopped clams with the juice. It really brings up the
flavor.
2 cloves garlic or more, chopped and divided
Red pepper flakes
Extra virgin olive oil
1/2 cup dry white wine (optional)
Fresh Italian parsley, chopped
1 to 2 chopped tomatoes.
Coarse salt, to taste.

Soak the clams in water and salt for one hour to purge: rinse well with
fresh water (omit this step if using just canned clams).
Heat some olive oil in a skillet over medium heat. Sauté red pepper
flakes and half the chopped garlic until golden, 1 to 2 minutes,
Add clams and wine to skillet. Cover with lid, cook over medium heat
for about 10 minutes or until clams are completely open. Discard any
unopened clams.
Meanwhile, cook Pasta according to package directions, reserving 1-2
ladles of cooking water. Remove the meat from about half of the
clams; discard empty shells and return meat to skillet. In a separate
skillet sauté remaining garlic in olive oil over medium heat for 2
minutes. Add tomatoes, season with salt and pepper. Simmer for 5
minutes. Add clams and wine to tomato sauce.
Drain pasta, toss with the sauce add some cooking water to obtain
desired consistency. Sprinkle with chopped parsley before serving.

HOLD THE CHEESE

Is it wrong to put grated cheese on seafood or a seafood pasta dish? Most Italians say that this is a no-no, it can overpower the delicate flavors of the fish.

Risotto a Frutta di Mare
Seafood Risotto

Vongole or small clams
Mussels, cleaned
Extra virgin olive oil
garlic, minced
Red pepper flakes to taste
1-2 cups short-grain rice (e.g. Arborio)
1/2-cup dry white wine
1 plum tomato, peeled, seeded, and diced (optional)
6 cups fish stock or clam broth
1/4-pound cleaned squid, bodies cut into rings and tentacles halved
1/4-pound medium shrimp, shelled and deveined
1-2 tablespoons unsalted butter
Italian parsley, minced

In a large bowl, soak the clams and mussels in water to cover with 1 tablespoon of salt for 30 minutes to purge them. Drain and rinse thoroughly. Place the clams and mussels in a pot with 1/2 cup of water, cover with a lid; cook over medium heat until they open. Remove from the heat, cool a few minutes, and shell; transfer to a bowl discarding the shells and any unopened clams and mussels. Strain the cooking juices through a cheesecloth-lined strainer into the bowl with the shelled clams and mussels.

Heat the olive oil in a heavy-bottomed sauté pan over a medium-high heat. Add the garlic and red pepper; heat until fragrant, about 30 seconds, stirring with a wooden spoon making sure that the garlic does not burn. Add the rice and cook 3 minutes, stirring constantly, Deglaze with wine. When the wine has evaporated, after about 2 minutes, add the tomato (optional); cook 5 minutes, stirring.

Heat the broth in a 2-quart saucepan. Add 1/2 cup of the broth to the rice and cook, stirring, until it is absorbed. Continue to cook the rice, stirring constantly and adding broth by the 1/2 cup whenever the liquid has been absorbed, about 15 minutes. Add the clams mussels, along with their reserved cooking liquid, then stir in the squid and shrimp; cook until the rice is done (al dente) a few more minutes, add broth as needed (you may not need all of the broth too much broth result in soggy rice rather than a risotto, Season with salt and freshly ground pepper, add the butter stir until creamy add parsley, and serve.

Contorni

Contorni/ Verdure

Broccoli Di Rapa con Peperoncino e Aglio
Cima di Rape con Patate
Carciofi I II
Spinaci Rifatti
Scarola in Padella
Cavolo "Cappuccio" alla Siciliana
Fagiolino con Pomadoro
Piselli con Prosciutto
Asparagi Gratinati
Arrosto di Vedure
Zucchini Fritti
Peperoni *I II III*
Patate Arrosto
Patata Schiacciata
Patata Dorato Fritte
Parmigiana di Melanzane
Giambotta
Fagioli all' Uccelletto
Frittella di Zucchinni
Pastella Per le Frittura
Fritto Misto di Vedure
Fritto di Cardoni / Cardi Fritti

Frittata
Frittata di Asparagi
Frittata con Zucchinni
Frittata con Spinaci
Frittata di Patate

Broccoli Di Rapa con Peperoncino e Aglio

Broccoli Rabe with Chili and Garlic

1 bunch Broccoli Rabe
1 1/2 Tbsp. olive oil
Coarse salt
1 oz. pancetta; chopped
3 anchovy filets; rinsed and finely chopped (Optional)
2 large Garlic cloves; chopped or sliced
Coarse salt and red pepper flakes to taste

Wash and Trim the bottom of the brocoli about 2-3 inches of the stem and discard. Then coarsely cut remaining greens, stems, and florets. Bring a pot of water to a boil with a little salt. Cook rabe in boiling water for five minutes or until tender. Do not overcook, then drain.

In a skillet over medium-low heat and add olive oil, pancetta, anchovies, and garlic. Cook until garlic is just beginning to lightly brown, about 5 minutes. The anchovies should melt into the oil. Increase heat to medium high. Add rabe to skillet and cook, stirring often until mixture is hot.

The addition of anchovies and oil cured black olives brings the dish to Sicily and wonderful memories of my aunt in her kitchen with fresh bread baking in a brick oven. With an amazing view of mount Etna.

Cima di Rape con Patate
Broccoli Rabe with Potatoes

1 bunch of Broccoli Rabe
2 Medium Potatoes or small reds
4 Tablespoons Extra Virgin Olive Oil
2 Cloves of Garlic, Minced
Coarse Salt
Red Pepper Flakes
Grated Italian Cheese (optional)

Clean and quarter the potatoes, and boil in salted water until they are fork tender. Clean the broccoli rabe, removing hard stems and yellowed leaves. Chop the rest into 2-inch pieces add the broccoli rabe. Cook until tender. Drain and set aside. In the same pot, heat the oil until sizzling, Add the garlic, allow to heat, then add the broccoli rabe, red pepper flakes and salt and pepper. Return the potatoes, smashing the potatoes a bit and cook a minute or two until everything is coated .Drizzle with extra oil and salt this dish is great both warm and room temperature. If desired add grated parmesan .

Cima di Rape con Patate is rustic country cooking at its best. Broccoli, Escarole, Spinach, or any type of green could also be substituted. Leave the skin on the potatoes or peel the potatoes before cooking them if you prefer. I remember my Mother's mother Angelina making dishes like this for my grandfather when I was a kid.

Carciofi con Acciuga
Artichokes with Anchovy Sauce

4 fresh artichokes
Salt and freshly ground pepper

Trim the stems of the artichokes, and slice 1 inch off the top of each. Remove and discard the tough outer leaves. Bring a pot of water to a boil add them to the boiling water and cook for 20 to 30 minutes. until center is cooked. Drain, season with salt and pepper.

Serve with a side of olive oil and vinegar salt and pepper in a little cup (with a bit of anchovy) to dip the leaves in. Just peel dip and eat.

Anchovy Sauce
1/2 cup extra- virgin olive oil
5 anchovies packed in salt, or caned rinsed, drained, and chopped
Juice of 1 lemon 1 or a Tablespoon red wine vinegar
Red pepper flakes (optional)
1 to 2 tablespoons water
Fresh minced Italian parsley
A few capers (optional)
Mix together and transfer to a small bowl, for dipping.

Carciofi Ripieni
Stuffed Artichokes

4 artichokes
1 cup bread crumbs
1/2 cup grated Pecorino-Romano Cheese
1 tablespoon parsley, chopped
1 to 2 cloves of garlic, minced
Coarse salt & freshly ground pepper to taste
4 to 6 tablespoons extra virgin olive oil

Combine bread crumbs, Pecorino-Romano Cheese, parsley, minced garlic, salt, pepper, and 2 tablespoons of the olive oil in a medium bowl. Mix together well.

Wash and trim artichokes. Cut the stems off chop in small pieces and add to bread mixture. Trim the tops of the artichokes. Spread leaves of each artichoke out and push stuffing in between them.

In a pot just large enough to fit the artichokes, add extra sliced garlic cloves and extra olive oil and the artichokes standing. Drizzle the some olive oil over the top of the artichokes.

Add water to reach half way up the sides of the artichokes. Cook on a medium heat. Cover and cook until the artichokes are tender, and a leaf is easily pulled out, about 35 to 45 minutes. If liquid is evaporating add a little more water. Drizzle a little of the liquid from the pot and add extra olive oil over the artichokes and serve.

Sometimes I like to add an anchovy filet chopped in small pieces to the stuffing it gives it a special taste. Try it!

Spinaci Rifatti
Recooked Spinach

2 pounds fresh spinach, washed well
2-3 tablespoons olive oil
2 medium cloves garlic, halved and crushed
Coarse Salt and pepper to taste
1/2 teaspoon crushed red pepper (optional)

Pick over the spinach, removing and discarding tough ribs, and coarsely chop the leaves. Heat it in a pot until it has wilted and drain it well, squeezing it to remove most of the water set aside.
Heat the oil in a sauté pan with the garlic, and once it begins to crackle, add the spinach, season with salt and pepper to taste, and when it is heated through it is done.

Scarola in Padella
Sautéed Escarole

2 tablespoons olive oil
3 garlic cloves, peeled and smashed
2 small heads escarole, trimmed, and leaves torn and washed well
Coarse salt
Red pepper flakes to taste

In a large skillet, heat oil over medium. Add garlic, and cook until fragrant and lightly golden not brown, about 1 minute. Stir in escarole;
season with salt and red pepper. Cook, stirring often, until tender, about 10 minutes. Place the escarole in a bowl and drizzle with olive oil. serve warm or at room temperature.

Add some boiled smashed potatoes for something different.

Cavolo "Cappuccio" alla Siciliana
Sicilian Stewed Cabbage

A green cabbage, quartered, cored, and cut up
1 to 2 clove garlic, peeled and chopped
2 tablespoon olive oil
1 to 1 1/2 cup crushed tomato
Salt to taste
Red pepper flakes to taste

Heat the olive oil in a pot. Add the garlic. Sauté for about a minute then add the tomatoes cook about ten minutes. Season with salt, add the cabbage until it has wilted, about 10 minutes, adding a little water if need be. Season with red pepper flakes. Simmer covered for another 1/2 hour over a very gentle heat, stirring often, and then adjust seasoning.

This very simple stewed cabbage is from my Sicilian grandmother Angelina, a great cook, she would also add cut up potatoes and cooked them together it truly was a meal by its self. She would also cook escarole or swiss chard the same way.

Fagiolino con Pomadoro
Green Beans with Tomatoes

Green beans, snip the ends (Italian broad beans if you can get them)
Fresh tomatoes or canned plum tomatoes chopped
Coarse salt
Extra virgin olive oil
1 to 2 cloves of garlic a small onion or both
Fresh basil or parsley

Put some olive oil in large heated pot. Add garlic and sauté lightly.
Add the tomatoes and basil. Cook slowly for about 20 minutes. In
another pot bring water to a boil. Snip the green bean ends and wash.
Add salt and beans to the boiling water. Cook for about 8 minutes.
Add drained beans to the tomato mixture and continue cooking until
they are tender. If the sauce becomes too thick add small amounts of
water. Cook until beans are tender.

In this case the beans taste better overcooked.
Add some cubed or sliced cooked potatoes for something different. With this
recipe, you can add a pinch of some dried oregano - just a pinch not to
overpower. This is like a hardy stew and can be eaten as such.
I have made this with broccoli rabe, escarole and cauliflower.

Piselli con Prosciutto
Peas with Prosciutto

2 to 3 tablespoons extra virgin olive oil
1/4 cup diced onion
1/4 cup diced prosciutto or Pancetta
2 cups fresh peas (you can substitute frozen)
Coarse Salt and fresh ground pepper to taste

In a medium skillet combine olive oil, onion, and prosciutto. Cook on medium for 4 to 5 minutes. Stir in peas and cook for 4 to 5 minutes more. Add salt and pepper and serve.

Asparagi Gratinati
Broiled Asparagus

medium-size asparagus spears
1/2 cup freshly grated cheese
fine plain or seasoned dry bread crumbs
2 cloves Garlic, chopped
3 tablespoons olive oil

Bring salted water to a boil in a large saucepan. Cut the tough woody bottoms of the stalks. Add the asparagus to the boiling water and cook until tender but still crisp, about 6 minutes. Drain well. Mix the cheese, bread crumbs, and garlic together until blended. Preheat the broiler. Arrange the asparagus stalks in a single later in a baking dish. Drizzle the asparagus with the oil and sprinkle an even layer of the bread crumb mixture over it. Broil about 4 minutes or until the bread crumb mixture is golden brown.

Arrosto di Verdure
Roasted Vegetables

An assortment of vegetables for example: eggplant, zucchini,
squash, bell peppers, mushrooms, red potatoes. Carrots or anything
you think will be a good combination
1 or 2 onions
2 to 4 cloves of garlic
Rosemary or thyme
Extra virgin olive oil
Coarse salt and fresh ground pepper

Preheat oven to 450 F.
Cut vegetables in similar sizes.
On a large cooking sheet, add garlic, salt, rosemary, and all
vegetables, except the mushrooms. Add olive oil, salt and pepper
then mix. Add more olive oil, if needed.Cook about 40 minutes,
turning occasionally or until golden brown and fork tender.
Add mushrooms and cook 10 minutes more.. taste for salt, and then
serve.

*A great vegetable side dish or as part of an antipasto. Example: Room
temperature roasted vegetables, prosciutto, and fresh mozzarella.*

Zucchini Fritti
Fried Zucchini

1 cup all-purpose flour
4 tablespoons bread crumbs
Salt and pepper, to taste
2 pounds zucchini, trimmed and cut into quarters lengthwise
Oil for frying
2 tablespoons chopped parsley

In a flat baking dish, stir together flour, bread crumbs, salt, and pepper. Coat zucchini in the breading mixture and set aside.
Fill a large skillet with enough oil to come 1/4-inch up the side. Heat oil to the smoking point, then, using tongs, carefully add the zucchini. Cook the zucchini until golden on all sides. Drain on paper towels. Season with more salt and pepper, if desired, then arrange on a platter. Sprinkle with parsley and serve.

Peperoni Arrosto
Roasted Peppers

4 large bell peppers in various colors
Olive oil
1 garlic clove, minced
Kosher salt and pepper, to taste

Grill or broil whole peppers on high heat until charred on all sides and flesh softens. Remove from grill and cover loosely with foil for 30 minutes. When cool enough to handle, remove, and discard the charred skin, seeds, and stems. Slice and arrange the peppers on a platter. In a small bowl, whisk together the olive oil and garlic. Drizzle over peppers add salt and pepper.

Peperonata Rustico
Rustic Peppers
Bell peppers any colors
1 or 2 onions
1 clove garlic
2-3 tomatoes (optional)
Olive oil
Salt and pepper to taste

Take bell peppers, seed them, and rib them. Thinly slice one or two onions, depending upon the number of peppers, crush a couple of tomatoes use caned plum tomatoes. Cut and sauté 1/2 of the onion in olive oil, and when it begins to brown add the remaining onion and the peppers. Cook covered for a few minutes over a medium flame, just long enough for the peppers and onion to wilt without browning. At this point remove the cover and cook, stirring gently, until the liquid evaporates. add the crushed tomatoes; when they have wilted.

Lower heat until completely cooked add salt and pepper to taste
(I prefer Red Pepper Flakes) the peperonata is ready, and can be
eaten hot, as a side dish, or cold on slices of toasted bread or a
bruschetta in a antipasti.

A Rustic Peperonata, or Peperonata Rustica: Peperonata is stewed peppers.

Peperoni e Uova
Peppers and Eggs

Olive oil
3 to 4 Italian frying peppers, seeded and cut into strips
1 onion, diced, a clove of garlic or both
Salt and pepper to taste
4 to 8 large eggs, beaten

Heat the oil in a large skillet over medium heat. Add the peppers and
onion and stir. Cover the skillet and let the vegetables steam until the
peppers soften. Season with salt and pepper .
In a large bowl, whisk the eggs and add to the peppers and onions.
Let the mixture set briefly and turn it with a large wooden spoon to
allow
the uncooked eggs to set. Stir again. Continue until the eggs are
done.

Enjoy this dish as it is or eat it in a sandwich made with crusty Italian bread.

Patate Arrosto
Roasted Potatoes

Roasting potatoes or small red
3 chopped garlic cloves
1 fresh rosemary sprig
extra virgin olive oil (more as needed)
Coarse salt and fresh ground pepper to taste

Wash, peel (I do not peel red potatoes) and cut your potatoes into
1/2-inch size cubes. Cut small red in half.
Preheat oven to 375- 400 F .
Pour olive oil into a baking dish and add in the rosemary and garlic.
Place the potatoes in the baking dish and mix with the olive oil mixture.
Season with a sprinkle of salt and pepper
Bake for about 35 minutes or until nice and brown. Stir half way through
and bake until the potatoes begin to brown evenly.
Depending on the size of the potatoes you will adjust the cooking time
and the seasoning.

That is, it you are done! but you must to wait until the potatoes are cooked.

*My dad would take whole potatoes and slip them into the embers of the fireplace
when we lit a fire: they would cook on their own and are wonderful with the meal,
especially when split in half and seasoned with olive oil and salt.*

Patata Schiacciata
Smashed Potatoes

Red or white skinned potatoes skins on
Extra virgin olive oil
4 to 6 large garlic cloves, minced
Coarse salt to taste
Ground black pepper
Chopped fresh parsley

Cook whole potatoes in very large pot of boiling water just until tender, about 40 minutes. Drain. Remove from pot add garlic and oil mixture sauté . Return potatoes and using fork, press each potato firmly in center to expose flesh and smash not mashed. Season with salt and pepper. Sprinkle with parsley and serve.

My grandmother would sauté (with the garlic and oil) cooked broccoli, spinach. Escarole even cauliflower, add potatoes and then smash them to incorporate and drizzle with extra virgin olive oil. A nice finish is toasted seasoned breadcrumbs on top.

Patata Dorato Fritte
Potato Croquettes

4 potatoes cooked and mashed or
4 cups leftover mashed potatoes
2 eggs
1/2 to 3/4 cup Italian grated cheese
Freshly ground nutmeg to taste
Fresh Italian Parsley chopped
Coarse salt and freshly ground pepper
Flour for dredging
Bread crumbs
Vegetable Oil for frying

Mash Potatoes until smooth Stir in 1 egg and the cheese season with salt pepper, parsley, and nutmeg until mixed and smooth, set aside (If potato mixture is two thin you can add some bread crumbs)

Beat 1 egg with 2 tablespoons water, salt, and pepper to make an egg wash. Pour the bread crumbs into another shallow bowl. Shape the potato mixture into 1-inch-by-3-inch logs. Gently roll the croquettes in the flour then in the egg, and finally in the bread crumbs, coating them thoroughly. Let the croquettes rest and refrigerated for about a half hour before frying.

In a large skillet add enough oil in the skillet to fry. Heat the oil to 350 F, and fry the croquettes, being careful not to overcrowd the pan. Once they are golden brown on all sides, remove with a slotted spoon and drain on paper towels. Add more parsley for garnish.

This is the simplest way, but you can add all kinds of things e.g. diced prosciutto, mozzarella, a sautéed diced onion.

Parmigiana di Melanzane
Eggplant with Parmesan and Tomatoes

1 to 2 large eggplants Salt and pepper
Vegetable oil for frying
2 tbsp olive oil, 2 cloves garlic chopped,
1/2 small onion chopped optional)
1 to 1 1/2 cup chopped tomatoes
1 large bunch fresh basil
1/2 to 3/4 cup Parmesan cheese, grated

Cut the eggplants into slices. Place in a large colander, sprinkle with salt and set aside for 30 minutes to remove any bitter juices.

Heat the vegetable oil in a large frying pan and, working in batches, fry the slices of eggplant until golden on each side. Remove and set aside. For a lighter dish, use grilled eggplant instead.

Place the olive oil, garlic and onion in a saucepan and sauté over a medium heat until the garlic or onion starts to lightly brown. Add the tomatoes, bring to a boil then simmer for 20 minutes. Season with salt and pepper and remove the pan from the heat.

Spread a large spoonful of the tomato sauce over the bottom of a dish. Lay enough eggplant slices in the dish to cover the bottom.

Spread some tomato sauce on the eggplant and Add a few leaves of basil and sprinkle a good amount the cheese.

Continue layering the eggplant, tomato sauce, basil and Parmesan cheese until the dish is full you should have at least three layers of eggplant and the top layer should be tomato sauce covered with cheese and basil. Serve at room temperature.

My opinion that this is the original eggplant parmigiana.
The ingredients in this recipe are simple: eggplant, olive oil, tomatoes, Parmesan, and fragrant fresh basil. The taste is simply delicious. One of my mother's favorite dishes to make
Parmigiana di Melanzane, or Eggplant Parmigiana, is a classic meat free Italian dish. It is easy to make and delicious with crusty Italian bread.

Giambotta
Mixed Stewed Vegetables

Extra virgin olive oil
Spanish onion, sliced
celery, diced
Fresh basil leaves, chopped
Plum tomatoes, peeled, seeded, and pureed
potatoes, peeled and cubed
Eggplant, cubed
Zucchini, cubed
Bell pepper, cored, seeded, and cut into thin strips
Coarse salt and Red pepper flakes to taste

In a large deep skillet heat the olive oil over medium heat. Add the onion, celery, and sauté until soft. Add the basil and sauté. Add the tomatoes, potatoes, eggplant, zucchini, water, and salt and pepper, and stir well. Cover and cook over low heat for 20 minutes. Add the pepper strips and cook for about 10 - 20 minutes or more, or until the vegetables are tender. (potatoes can be pre-cooked, cut, and then added for the last 10 minutes)

Giambotta, like the French ratatouille, is a hearty vegetable stew of eggplant, zucchini, tomatoes, potatoes etc. The slow cooking blends the flavors of all the vegetables.

Fagioli all' Uccelleto
Tuscan Beans

8 oz of dry cannellini or cranberry beans
1 to 1 1/2 cup peeled tomatoes (pureed)
1/2 cup of extra virgin olive oil
2 cloves of garlic (chopped)
Fresh sage or fresh rosemary
Salt and pepper (I prefer red pepper flakes)

Soak the beans overnight for 12 hours in 2 quarts of water. Drain and cook in water at low temperature so that the beans do not break apart. Remove from the stove before they are fully cooked in a heavy pan, heat the olive oil, and chopped garlic until garlic is almost translucent in color, then add the sage leaves and cook until the leaves are softened. Slowly stir in the pureed tomatoes and cook for 10 minutes. Add the beans, mixing thoroughly and cook for 15 minutes. Add salt and pepper to taste and serve with a drizzle of olive oil.

The more these beans rest and reheated they are even better. Make them with sausages it is extremely tasty: The people of Tuscany are known in Italy as mangiafagioli, or bean eaters.

Frittella di Zucchinni
Zucchini Fritters

3 or 4 small zucchinis, coarsely grated
minced garlic or small onion chopped
2 large eggs
1/2 cup grated cheese
1/2 tsp baking powder
Flour
Salt & pepper to taste
2 Tb chopped parsley or basil
Oil for frying

Grate zucchini and place in a colander or strainer and let drain for at least 1/2 hour. Squeeze dry to let some of the water out and place all the ingredients in a mixing bowl except the flour mix until smooth; add flour in small amounts until mixture resembles a very thick pancake batter, if too thick add a little milk or water.
Heat 1/2 cup oil in a frying pan 350 F. Drop 1 to 2 heaping tablespoons in the hot oil fry until lightly browned turn gently about 2-3 minutes on each side or until cooked through.
Drain and serve

Also, can be served at room temperature Great in antipasto

Pastella Per le Frittura
Batter for Frying

1 cup flour
1 cup milk, beer, or sparkling water
1 - 2 eggs
1 to 2 cloves garlic chopped
1 tablespoon fresh parsley or basil chopped
Salt and Pepper to taste
1 tsp tomato paste for color and taste (optional)

Beat together until smooth with the consistency of a pancake batter Italian Fried Vegetables also known as Fritto Misto di Verdure is a recipe using a variety of vegetables bathed in a creamy batter and fried to golden brown. They are so delicious that people devour them without realizing what they are eating. You can use many different vegetables; Italian Fried Vegetables are often made and served at room temperature at a meal.

The secret is in the "pastella" or batter. The consistency should be thick enough to cling to a fork without completely running off. If the batter becomes too runny, add a little more flour. If the batter becomes too thick, add a little more beer, or sparkling water.

In medium bowl, mix flour into eggs, then add milk, beer or sparkling mineral water. Stir continuously and add salt and pepper to taste.

If batter is too thick, add a little more milk ,beer or sparkling mineral water. If batter is too runny, add a little more flour. You can even make a simple batter with just flour and water salt pepper an addition of baking powder or a pinch of yeast, also you can separate the eggs adding the yolks and then fold in beaten egg whites to lighten the batter up.

Try all combinations but just keep the flavoring light so you do not mask the taste of the vegetables you are frying.

Fritto Misto di Vedure
Italian Fried Vegetables

In a deep skillet or fryer Heat cooking oil at 375 F. Wash vegetables, cut into bite-size pieces. Par boil most vegetables except zucchini and zucchini flowers and dry with paper towel. Set aside.
Dip vegetables into batter and completely coat.
Carefully place vegetables into hot oil and cook on all sides until light brown. Drain on paper towels and serve.

Depending on the season you can use different vegetables e.g. broccoli, cauliflower, asparagus , string beans (all pre-cooked but slightly firm) and frozen artichoke hearts defrosted.

Fritto di Cardoni/Cardi Fritti
Fried Cardoon I

Peel the strings from the cardoons, cut them into 3-inch pieces. Cardoon are related to the artichoke. The thistle it produces is not edible, but the stalks, which look like overgrown celery, are delicious and have a taste similar to artichoke hearts. To clean cardoons: Pull apart stalks of cardoon. With a sharp knife, remove any leaves that are spiny, and the heavy fibers that run like celery fibers down the backs of the stalks. Slice into 3- 4-inch pieces. Boil them in salted water until fork tender, drain and cool, dip them in the batter (one to two pieces together if small), and fry them in the oil. Drain.

My mother always made them when in season. They were so tempting to pick on just after being fried. They are delicious as part of an antipasto or as an accompaniment to a second plate.

Fried Cardoon II
3/4 cup bread crumbs
1/4 cup all-purpose flour
2 tablespoons parmigiano cheese
2 egg
vegetableoil for frying

Cook cardoon in generous amount of boiling water until soft, about 20 to 30 minutes. Drain and set aside In a large bowl mix together bread crumbs, flour and cheese. Beat eggs. Dip cooked cardoons in egg, then in flour ,bread crumbs and cheese mixture. Fry until golden.

Thanksgiving or Christmas holidays always had fried cardoon on the table.

Verdure

In Italy most of the sides are vegetables served in the simplest ways. Verdure are greens that are blanched or boiled, drained, cooled, and seasoned with salt, pepper, olive oil and lemon juice (or quite rarely vinegar).
Some of the vegetables of choice are chicory, string beans, fava, arugula (rocket), spinach, broccoli, cauliflower, broccoli rabe and asparagus.

Beans: Soak and boil your beans, drain them, and season them with olive oil, salt, pepper, and freshly minced parsley.
Potatoes: peel and boil the potatoes until they are fork-tender, cut them and season them with olive oil, vinegar , Corse salt, freshly ground pepper, and parsley. Served at room temperature
Beets: slice them thinly, season the mixture with salt, pepper, olive oil, vinegar, and parsley or basil.

The Frittata

Frittata, a close relative of the omelet in which the eggs are seasoned and beaten, then poured into a skillet with some sort of filler, and cooked until one side is done and the other is firm. The frittata is then flipped and cooked until the other side until it is done. (my choice is to put it under the broiler for 2 to 3 minutes).

Beat seasoned eggs (one-and-a-half to two eggs per person) to incorporate some air into them, this will make for a fluffier frittata. Pour the eggs into the skillet over vegetables, meats cheeses or any combo, even left-over pasta, that have been sautéed, with seasonings. A brisk shake to distribute them evenly though the filler, and let the frittata cook, without stirring, until the top begins to firm up. All you have to do is place an empty inverted plate over the pan and flip. Flip it upside-down .and slide it back in the pan. It should not be runny, nor should it be bone dry. if your skillet has heatproof handles you can slip it into the broiler for a few minutes once the top begins to set. Slice the frittata into wedges as you might a pizza before you serve it. "Rustic cuisine," at its best Quick, easy, and very tasty Frittata can be eaten either hot or cold. Cut into wedges they make excellent antipasto. They are also perfect for light meals, with bread or a contorni.

Prepare the filler, usually by sautéing it, and have it ready in the skillet.

Frittata di Asparagi

Asparagus Omelet

1/2-pound asparagus, trimmed and cut into 1-inch lengths-blanched
6 eggs
1/2 cup freshly grated Parmesan
Salt and pepper
4 tablespoons olive oil or butter
1 small red onion, minced or garlic chopped

In a saucepan of boiling salted water, blanch the asparagus for 1 or 2 minutes, or until just tender. Drain.

In a bowl, whisk the eggs with 1/3 cup of the Parmesan and salt and pepper. In a 1/2- inch nonstick skillet over medium heat, warm the oil or butter until hot. Add the onion and cook, stirring occasionally, for 3 minutes. Add the asparagus pieces and cook, stirring, for 1 minute more. Pour the beaten eggs into the skillet, reduce the heat to low, and cook the mixture, covered, for 8 minutes, or until the eggs are almost set.

Sprinkle the top of the frittata with the remaining cheese. Place under the broiler about 4 inches from the heat and cook for 1 to 2 minutes, or until the eggs are set. Cut into wedges and serve.

Sometimes I include small cubed mozzarella pieces into the egg mixture before adding to the skillet.

Fritata is eaten for lunch or supper and served as a side, It makes a hearty and tasty meatless meal.

Frittata con Zucchinni

Zucchini Omelet

6 eggs, beaten
1-ounce Pecarino-Romano, freshly grated
Freshly ground black pepper, Coarse salt to taste
olive oil
1/2 cup zucchini, small cubed
1 cup red potatoes, cubed (I pre-cook the potatoes)
1/2 small red onion sliced thin
parsley leaves, chopped
Coarse salt and fresh ground pepper to taste

In medium size bowl, mix together eggs, cheese, salt, and pepper to taste. Heat non-stick, oven safe sauté pan over medium high beat. Add 1 tsp olive oil. Add potatoes to pan and sauté for 2 to 3 minutes. Remove potatoes and set aside.
Heat 1 tsp olive oil over medium high heat sauté onion, add the zucchini slices and sauté for 2 minutes.
Return the potatoes to the pan. Add the egg mixture into the pan and stir. Cook for 4 to 5 minutes, the egg mixture should be set on the bottom and begin to set up on top.
Place pan into oven and broil for 3 to 4 minutes, until lightly browned and fluffy. Sprinkle with parsley. Serve warm or at room temperature.

Frittata con Spinaci

Spinach Frittata

4 to 6 eggs
2 to 4 tablespoons milk or heavy cream (optional)
Fresh spinach cooked and drained (you can use frozen but drained well)
1 heaping tablespoon flour (optional flour helps absorb liquid)
Grated Italian cheese to taste
1 clove garlic, chopped
Olive oil
A pinch nutmeg
Fresh Parsley or basil
Salt and fresh ground pepper to taste

Wash the spinach dry well then heat it in a pot with just the water left on the leaves after it drains until it wilts; squeeze it dry, coarsely chop it, and sauté with the garlic, oil, and a pinch of nutmeg. Remove and set aside. Beat the eggs, cream in a bowl. Stir in the flour, and cheese, season with salt and pepper. Heat oil and garlic in a skillet, and when it begins to lightly brown, return spinach an add the egg mixture, shaking the skillet briskly to settle things. Cook the frittata until the bottom is done and the top begins to firm up, then flip or put under broiler and cook it a few minutes more before serving it. It can be served either hot or at room temperature.

Almost any vegetable sautéed with garlic and a tablespoon of minced parsley or basil are excellent as are broccoli florets (steamed for a few minutes, then sautéed).
A spinach frittata is one of the most classic simple dishes you will encounter in Italy and you may see it on antipasto platters like most frittata.

Frittata di Patate

Potato Omelet

1 cup red potatoes, cubed
4 to 6 eggs
2 to 4 Tablespoons cream or milk
1/3 to 1/2 cup parmesan or other grating cheese
Salt and fresh ground pepper
4 tablespoons olive oil
1 small red onion or garlic clove, minced
2 Tbsp. minced fresh parsley, basil, or both

Heat non-stick, oven safe sauté pan over medium high heat. Add 2 tablespoons olive oil to pan. Cube or dice potatoes Add potatoes to pan and sauté until done (you can par-boil the potatoes and then sauté in olive oil) Remove potatoes and set aside.
Heat 2 tablespoons olive oil over medium high heat. Add the onion and garlic and sauté for 2 minutes. Return the potatoes to the pan. Pour the egg mixture into the pan. Cook for 4 to 5 minutes, the egg mixture should be set on the bottom and begin to set up on top.
Place pan into oven and broil for 3 to 4 minutes, until lightly browned and fluffy. Sprinkle with parsley or basil.
Serve warm or at room temperature.

I use the same recipe with cauliflower even broccoli a nice change for lunch or supper. It makes a hearty and tasty meatless meal.

Insalata

Insalata Verde /Green Salad
Fennel Salad
Fennel Salad with Oranges
Neapolitan Cauliflower Salad
White Bean and Tuna Salad
Potato Salad and Green Beans

Insalata Crude -- Raw Salads
The raw salads, are, as you might expect, a mix of salad greens
(lettuce, arugula, endive, and so on) tossed together. Everything that
goes into the salad is green; you rarely come across other things in a
traditional salad. What you will occasionally find is a sliced hard-
boiled egg or carrots thinly sliced (In Sicily they use grated carrots)
A tomato salad made with sun-ripened tomatoes. Cut them. Add if
you like some red onion sliced thin or minced, olive oil, salt, pepper,
and minced parsley or basil. Serve with fresh bread.
Roman Salads also include part cooked and part fresh, all made of
mixture of vegetables and may include cooked meat or fish and
lightly dressed.

Insalata Verde
Green Salad

Salad greens
Extra virgin olive oil
Red wine vinegar or fresh lemon juice (optional)
Coarse salt and freshly ground pepper
Garlic (optional)

Rinse the greens very well. Let dry. Use paper towels to squeeze dry the salad, or spin it.

Slice the garlic clove in half or smash it and rub the sides of the salad bowl thoroughly. Pour olive oil over the salad mix. Pour it a few times around the bowl about 3 tablespoons.

Add a little of the red wine vinegar or fresh lemon. This is optional and you do not have to use it.

Add a dash of kosher salt. Mix it all very well and make sure to get the salad to rub the sides which will pick up a slight garlic flavor. Serve with freshly ground pepper.

Most Italians often put the olive oil and vinegar on the table. Italians eat their salads after or with the second dish. Escarole hearts and chicory are also great in a salad.

Insalata di Finocchio

Fennel Salad

1 bulb fennel (Fronds removed and saved for soup)
1 lemon
Extra virgin Olive oil
Coarse salt to taste
Fresh cracked black pepper

Cut fennel bulb in half lengthwise. Lay halves cut-side down and use
a sharp knife to slice crosswise as thinly as possible (or, use a
mandolin) Put fennel in a medium bowl. Drizzle with olive oil
squeeze lemon add salt to taste sprinkle with fresh parsley.

Great in an antipasto!
The addition of thinly sliced oranges especially blood oranges is a wonderful
treat and a burst of sunshine to any winter meal.

Insalata di Finoccho e Arange

Sicilian Fennel Salad with Oranges, Arugula, and Black Olives

3 blood or navel oranges
Extra-virgin olive oil
Red wine vinegar (I do not always use vinegar sometimes I use
lemon or just olive oil and salt)
Coarse Salt
Freshly ground black pepper
Arugula or chicory, cleaned and trimmed
Fennel bulbs cored, and, trimmed
Oil-cured black olives

Trim off and discard peel and all the white pith from oranges, then slice crosswise into thin rounds and set aside. Mix together extra-virgin olive oil and red wine vinegar in a large salad bowl, then season to taste with salt and freshly ground black pepper. Tear arugula into large pieces and arrange in the salad bowl. Slice fennel bulbs into long strips. Toss salad just before serving, adjust seasonings, then arrange orange slices and black olives on top.

In Sicily, this salad is traditionally prepared with wild chicory, a slightly peppery, tender- leafed green. Substitute with arugula if you cannot find wild chicory.
Wonderful to serve after the second plate, it is nice and tart and refreshing to the pallet especially after fish.

Insalata di Cavolfiore
Neapolitan Cauliflower Salad

6 tablespoons extra-virgin olive oil
2 tablespoons wine vinegar
6 anchovy fillets, mince
Dried oregano, crushed to taste
3/4 cup coarsely chopped oil cured black olives
1/4 cup capers, drained and dried, chopped
1 1/2 cups roasted red bell pepper strips
2 cloves garlic, minced
1/4 cup finely chopped Italian parsley
Coarse salt and freshly ground pepper

1 large cauliflower head, trimmed of stem and tough outer leaves, cut into 1-inch florets bring a large pot of salted water to boil and the cauliflower. Cook 5 or 6 minutes until the florets are tender, drain and run under cold water to stop cooking. Drain well and pat dry with paper towels.

In a large bowl, combine the oil, vinegar and anchovies. Whisk to make a smooth sauce. Then add the oregano, olives, capers, peppers, garlic and parsley and stir so the olives and peppers are well-coated. Set aside.

Add the cauliflower, salt and freshly ground pepper to taste. Toss lightly. Leave at room temperature for several hours to allow flavors to develop. If made one or 2 days ahead, refrigerate but then bring the salad to room temperature.

Traditional in Naples and Campania.

Insalta di Tonno e Fagioli
White Bean and Tuna Salad

2 Cups Cooked Cannellini Beans, you can use caned but drain very well

2 6 oz. Cans Italian tuna packed in olive oil (no substitute)

1 Small red onion, sliced very thin

2 Stalks celery, chopped

Capers (optional)

Dressing
Lemon juice or red wine vinegar

Extra virgin olive oil

Salt and Pepper

Fresh Parsley, chopped

Mix together the dressing ingredients. Place the beans, onion, celery, and olives in a bowl. Drain the tuna, and lightly crumble it into the bowl with the beans. Pour the dressing over the bean mixture and toss, being careful not to break up the tuna too much. A few capers are a great addition. Let rest refrigerated for a least 1 hour.

Cooked string beans or Italian flat beans are a great substitute for the cannellini beans. This salad makes a wonderful antipasto or a light lunch. Popular summer dish in Naples and Campania.

Insalata di Patata con Fagioli
Potato Salad and Green Beans

Potatoes, peeled (red potatoes are a good choice even not peeled)
Fresh green beans
Red onion chopped or sliced thin
Fresh parsley, chopped
Extra virgin olive oil
Red Wine vinegar to taste (optional)
Coarse salt and freshly ground pepper

Bring a large pot of salted water to a boil. Plunge green beans in and
cook until just done but still slightly firm. Remove with a strainer
and set aside in a large bowl. Bring the water back to boiling and
drop in the potatoes. Boil, and cook until potatoes are tender but still
firm, about 12 to 15 minutes, depending on the potato. Check by
piercing a potato with a small sharp knife. Drain potatoes and cool.
Slice and then add to the bowl with the beans. Mix the potatoes,
parsley vinegar, olive oil, chopped onions or thinly sliced add salt
and fresh ground pepper to taste. Refrigerate until needed, serve at
room temperature.

This salad is great in the summer especially with grilled chicken and sausages.

Pane

Pane, Pizza, Focaccia

Pane Rustico
Ciabatta
Pasta per Pizza
Pizza Sauce
Pizza Margherita
Pizza Fritta
Pasta di Patate or Focaccia
Focaccia
Focaccia al Rosmarino
Pizza di Cipolla
Pane di Lardo
Pizza Stromboli
Sfincione Di Palermo
Pizza Rustica
Pizza Scarola
Pane di Pasqua
Garlic Knots
Zeppole
Calzone
Breadcrumbs
Garlic Toasts

*Bread is one of the most changeable Italian foods:
In different areas you will find different flours or
combinations of flours, some use salt and others do
not, some shape their breads into loaves, others
round, some brush their bread with oil, some dry it...
And that is just a beginning.*

Panne, Pizza, Focaccia

These are some of the simpler dough recipes for bread and pizza. You can start out with a sponge, or a Biga which brings the dough to a higher level. Most of the time I use the simple ones they are basic and can be used for almost anything, Bread, Pizza, Focaccia, Calzone, stuffed breads etc.

Biga
The sponge

A biga, or starter. adds flavor and extra leavening power to bread dough.

3/4 teaspoon active dry yeast
3 1/2 cups unbleached bread flour
1/2 cup warm water
1 1/4 cups cold water

Place the warm water in a small bowl and sprinkle the yeast over the top. Let stand until yeast has dissolved and is foamy, about 15 minutes.

Measure flour into a large bowl. Make a well in the center and pour in the yeast mixture and cold water. Use a sturdy spoon to mix it together until sticky and difficult to stir, but nevertheless thoroughly combined. Cover and allow to ferment for 24 hours in the refrigerator before using.

Store in the refrigerator for up to 2 weeks. To use, rinse a measuring cup in cool water, scoop out the amount of starter needed and bring to room temperature.

Pane Rustico
Rustic Bread

2 cups lukewarm water
1 package active dry yeast
5 to 5 1/3 cups bread flour
1/2 tsp sugar
2 tablespoons extra-virgin olive oil
1 teaspoon salt
1 egg, lightly beaten
sesame seeds

Stir the yeast into 1/2 cup of the warm water. Let proof. Combine 5 cups flour, sugar and salt in a large bowl then add the yeast mixture and the remaining water and olive oil mix until a dough starts to form, adding more flour or water (as much as you need.-this is important). Knead 7 minutes. Transfer dough to lightly floured surface and knead by hand for 4 to 5 minutes, or until a smooth, firm, elastic dough is formed.

Transfer the dough to a lightly oiled bowl and coat the dough with a coating of oil, cover the bowl with plastic wrap and a towel on top set aside to proof in a warm draft-free place for 1 1/2 hours or until doubled in size.

Remove the plastic wrap, punch down and flatten the rounded dough. Roll the dough up tightly, sealing the seam well after each roll. The dough should be elongated and oval-shaped, with tapered and rounded ends.

Preheat the oven lined with a baking stone to 425 F.

Place the dough on a baker's peel or on an inverted baking sheet heavily dusted with flour or corn meal.

Allow the formed dough to proof, loosely covered with a floured cloth, for 30 minutes, or until doubled in size.

Brush the dough with the egg and sprinkle the sesame seeds over the top. Using a razor blade or sharp knife, slash the dough lengthwise about 1/4-inch deep. Spray the dough generously with water from a water bottle and place in the pre heated oven on the baking stone. Immediately close the oven and bake for 5 minutes. Open the oven door and spray the dough again with the water bottle. Close the oven door and bake for an another 3 to 5 minutes before spraying the dough for a third time (the spraying of the dough will ensure a crisp golden-brown crust).

Bake the dough for a total of 45 minutes, or until a hollow thud is heard when tapping the bottom of the bread. Allow the bread to cool before slicing.

You can bake this on a baking sheet covered with parchment paper. The recipe calls for squirting this with a spray bottle of water in 3-5minute intervals when it first begins baking, Bake at 450 F until golden brown.

For olive bread: Add 1 cup of flavorful dried oil cured black olives or Kalamata olives, pitted, and chopped, dust with flour then mix into the dough then shape them into forms. Cover and let rise for 1 hour. Transfer to baking sheets rubbed with olive oil. Bake at 450 F until golden brown.

Ciabatta

"Slipper" Bread

The sponge
1/2 teaspoon active dry yeast
1/3 cup room-temperature water
1 cup bread flour

The bread
1/2 teaspoon active dry yeast
1/4 teaspoon sugar
2/3 cup water (110 F)
1 tablespoon olive oil
2 cups bread flour
1 1/2 teaspoons salt

The sponge
In a small bowl stir together yeast and warm water and let stand 5
minutes. In a bowl stir together yeast mixture, room-temperature
water, and flour and stir. Cover bowl with plastic wrap. Let sponge
stand at cool room temperature at least 12 hours and up to 1 day.
The bread
In bowl blend together, sponge, water, oil, and flour knead 7
minutes. Add salt and need 4 minutes more. Scrape dough into an
oiled bowl and cover with plastic wrap. Let dough rise at room
temperature until doubled in bulk, about 1 hours. (Dough will be
sticky and full of air bubbles.)

Have ready a rimless baking sheet and 2 well-floured 12- by 6-inch sheets parchment paper. Turn dough out onto a well-floured work surface and cut in half. Transfer each half to a parchment sheet and form into an irregular oval about 9 inches long. Dimple loaves with floured fingers and dust tops with flour. Cover loaves with a dampened kitchen towel. Let loaves rise at room temperature until almost doubled in bulk, 1 1/2 to 2 hours.

 The ciabatta does require a simple sponge, but it takes only a few minutes to put together the day before making the bread. Though the dough for ciabatta is very wet and sticky, resist the temptation to add more flour.

Pasta per Pizza
Basic Pizza Dough

Sponge
1 package (2 1/2 teaspoons) active dry yeast
1 cup lukewarm water
1/2 teaspoon sugar
2 tablespoon flour
Dough
1 sponge (recipe above)
4 1/2 cups (approx.) flour
1 cup (approx.) lukewarm water
2 tablespoons olive oil
1 tablespoon salt

In a large bowl combine all sponge ingredients. Cover and let sit 15 minutes. Sponge mixture should look foamy. If it does not look foamy start over with new yeast.

To make the dough, add 4 cups of flour into the bowl with the sponge mixture. Add 1 cup water, oil, and salt. Mix well either by hand or in a mixer with a dough hook. The dough will be sticky. Remove and knead with both hands for 5 to 6 minutes. Add more water or flour if needed to have a ball of dough. Transfer the dough to a lightly oiled bowl and coat the dough with a coating of oil, cover the bowl with plastic wrap and a towel on top and set aside to proof in a warm draft-free place for 1 1/2 hours or until doubled in size. Remove dough from bowl and place on a floured surface. Knead dough again and divide, shape each into a flat disk, about 1/4-inch thick. You can use a rolling pin but do not press hard on the dough. You can press out with your fingers on a cookie sheet that has been sprayed with nonfat cooking spray or use 1 tablespoon of cornmeal distributed evenly on the cookie sheet. Lay the dough on the cornmeal before adding toppings. This will help prevent sticking. Crusts can be topped with the toppings of your choice.

Pizza Sauce

1 28 ounce can crushed tomatoes
1/2 teaspoon dried oregano (optional)
2 Tablespoons extra virgin olive oil
2 cloves minced garlic cloves
Salt and Pepper to taste

Heat the olive oil over medium heat in medium saucepan.
Add the minced garlic cloves and stir often for 2 to 3 minutes over low heat until lightly browned. Do not burn the garlic.
Add in the can of crushed tomatoes, reduce heat to simmer and cook for about 15 minutes stirring occasionally. When ready remove from heat and cool slightly.
Your sauce is ready for the pizza. Freeze any left over for next time. This is a sauce you can use on any pizza with any topping of your choice that needs a tomato base.

I like San Marzano tomatoes on the Pizza, simple (semplice) no cooking just drained and crushed, for a very fresh taste.

Pizza Margherita
Pizza with Tomatoes, Mozzarella, and Basil

1 recipe Pizza Dough
1 2/3 cups grated or sliced mozzarella cheese
2/3-1 cup Marinara Sauce or to taste
3 garlic cloves, finely minced (in Naples they do not use garlic)
2 tablespoons freshly grated Parmesan (optional)
1 tablespoon extra-virgin olive oil
Oregano or fresh basil

Preheat the oven to 450 F.
On a floured surface, roll out the pizza dough into 1/4 -inch-thick round. Fit the dough into an oiled pizza pan or arrange it on an oiled heavy baking sheet. Sprinkle the dough with the mozzarella and spoon the marinara sauce over it, leaving a small border. Top with the garlic and   then sprinkle on the Parmesan. Drizzle with the olive oil.
Bake the pizza in the lower third of the oven for 15 to 20 minutes, or until the cheese is melted and the crust is golden brown.

This popular pizza is testimony to the enduring appeal of fresh tomato sauce, mozzarella, and tender basil.

Pizza Fritta

Fried Pizza Dough

Pizza dough
1 cup vegetable oil

In a deep-frying pan heat oil (350 F -375 F)
Break off pieces of dough.
Stretch dough without tearing it to your desired shape (irregular or disk shaped)
Place in hot oil, cook until done (around 3-5 min and turning once).
Place on paper towel and let drain
Serve plain or top with any savory topping for example, Sauce, cheese, garlic oil, salt or whatever you like.
For sweet - Sprinkle with powdered sugar, granulated sugar, or flavored sugars e.g., Cinnamon sugar.

I just love them as is, with a little coarse salt. My Grandmother use to make this treat when she was preparing pizza or bread. Make with any leftover or unused pizza dough.

Potato Pizza or Focaccia Dough

1 large chef 1or 2 small potatoes
1 Tablespoon. Active dry yeast I package dry
3/4 cup. lukewarm water
2 1/2 cups flour,
1 teaspoon. salt
1 Tablespoon extra-virgin olive oil

Boil the potato in water to cover until tender, 20-30 minutes; drain and peel. In a small bowl dissolve, the yeast in 3/4 cup water and let stand until slightly foamy on top, about 15 minutes. In a large bowl stir together the 2 1/2 cups flour and the salt. Pass the peeled potato through a ricer then into the bowl and form the mixture into a mound. Make a well in the center of the mound and add the yeast mixture to the well. Using a fork and stirring in a circular motion, gradually pull the flour and potato into the yeast mixture. Continue stirring until a dough comes together. Lightly flour a work surface with some of the extra flour and transfer the dough to it. Using the heel of your hand, knead the dough until it is smooth and elastic, about 10 minutes. Form the dough into a ball.

Pour a little oil in a bowl and place the dough in it cover with plastic wrap and then a towel. Let rise at room temperature until doubled, 1-2 hours. Turn the dough out onto a surface dusted with flour. Punch the dough down. At this point you may either let the dough rise once again, or you may roll out into the desired shape.

My mother's cousin Angie would make a fabulous potato dough pizza with an onion topping Sicilian style. What a great cook she was.

Focaccia Dough

Sponge
1/2 cup warm water
2 teaspoons fresh active dry yeast
1 teaspoon sugar

Dough
1 1/2 cups warm water
4 tablespoons olive oil, divided
3/1/2 to 4 cups high gluten or all-purpose flour
1 teaspoon Coarse sea salt or kosher salt

In a large bowl, combine water, yeast, and sugar. Whisk to mix well. Cover with plastic wrap for 5 minutes. If yeast is foamy, continue. Stir in the other 1 1/2 cups water and 3 tablespoons olive oil, and then stir in flour and salt. You may use an electric mixer with a bread hook or mix well with a large spoon. Mix until dough is well blended and slightly sticky. Remove and, if hand-blended, knead for 5 to 7 minutes (add extra flour if dough is too moist). Transfer dough to a large bowl, coat with 1 tablespoon olive oil and cover with a plastic wrap. Let rest for 1 1/2 hours. Place dough on a lightly oiled or floured 10 x 15- inch Baking sheet. Take the risen dough and spread it enough to completely cover the baking sheet, dimpling the surface by pressing down on it using your fingertips. cover with clean cloth and let sit for 30 minutes. Preheat your oven to 400 F
Take the remaining oil and beat it lightly with a little water to make an emulsion; brush this emulsion over the focaccia and sprinkle it with coarse sea salt, Rosemary, or any other topping. Bake the focaccia in a low rack until it is light golden brown, turning it 180 degrees when it is half-cooked, then continue cooking until done. Remove it and let it cool. Do not let it over brown.

Focaccia al Rosmarino
Flatbread with Rosemary

Add 1 tablespoon minced fresh rosemary leaves to the dough and
Fresh rosemary sprigs for garnish
Focaccia is one of Italy's great rustic flatbreads. Depressions are made
in focaccia to trap a variety of wonderful toppings - cheese, coarse
salt or, or in this case, rosemary, and olive oil.
It is also a wonderful base for a sandwich, just slice and fill.

Pizza di Cipolla
Onion Pie

Medium Onions, Peeled and Thinly Sliced
Tablespoons Olive Oil
Pancetta (optional)
Rosemary

In a heavy frying pan, heat the olive oil and add the diced Pancetta.
Cook over medium heat until the Pancetta begins to brown. Scoop the
pancetta from the pan and set aside in a bowl, leaving the oil in the
pan. Add the sliced onions to the pan and stir well to coat with the oil.
Cook over medium low heat 10 to 15 minutes, or until the onions are
very soft and just beginning to brown set aside.
Preheat oven to 425 F. Punch down dough and place on a 13 x 9-inch
oiled baking sheet, forming into an oval or rectangle. Dimple the top
with your finger tips and then evenly spread the onions across the top.
Sprinkle with the pancetta pieces, and then sprinkle with coarse salt
and rosemary. Bake about 20 to 25 minutes or until golden brown.

*This bread is great baked crisp, and the onions should be cut paper thin for the
topping. I used a mandolin to cut my onions and then tossed them with olive oil,
salt, and lots of cracked black pepper before arranging them on my pizza dough.*

Pane di Lardo
Lard Bread

Basic bread dough
Good rendered lard (Olive oil can be substituted)
Salami, prosciutto, pancetta etc. cut in small chunks
Grated Cheese
Provolone (Caccacavalo) (optional)
Fresh cracked black pepper
Dried Thyme (optional)

Let the dough rise until it double. Punch down and roll out into a large square (about 12" x 15" you need to use your judgment here). Spread on some lard (I have no idea on the amount) and sprinkle with a lot of fresh cracked pepper. Add 1/4 pound each of chopped up salami and pancetta and a little chopped up prosciutto if you like. Sprinkle with coarsely grated pecorino romano or parmigiano. Roll up into a tube and twist (you can make two small ones). Grease sheet pan with lard and form a ring, Seam on the bottom. Let rise for an hour. When ready, place in oven at 375 - 400 F until the top is nice and brown and looks ready. This normally takes about 1 hour.
Let bread cool. Place in a paper bag (not plastic) and leave it for the following day (do not refrigerate) It really needs to rest to get flavor.

Savory Neapolitan Bread. "this bread is addictive" Serve sliced or in broken off pieces.
There is really no substitute for good rendered lard (it gives it an amazing flavor) but I have used extra virgin olive oil instead. You can add fresh herbs if you like (e.g. Rosemary or thyme) Have fun with this bread.

Pizza Stromboli
Rolled Pizza

Basic Bread or Pizza dough

Filling
prosciutto, pepperoni, hard salami
sliced mozzarella cheese
sliced provolone cheese (optional)

Take bread or pizza dough and flatten it out in a rectangle the length of the cookie sheet and 8 inches wide.

Layer filling from one end to the other along the longest part of the dough. Beginning with the meat, layer all the way down, then add next layer using mozzarella cheese, then layer meat, provolone, and finish with a layer of hard salami.

Fold or roll the dough as to enclose all ingredients (tuck in ends). Put seam facing down on a very lightly greased or use parchment paper on cookie sheet.

Poke a few holes with fork in roll to allow for steam to escape.

Brush with egg wash (I like to add some sesame seeds on top)

Preheat oven, bake at 425 F degrees till slightly brown about 30 to 40 minutes or more depending on the size. Remove and allow to cool Serve room temperature.

Stromboli can be made with all kinds of fillings e.g. broccoli rabe instead of the meat or even sausage and peppers or any combination you can think of, try everything. Enjoy!

Sfincione Di Palermo
Sicilian Pizza from Palermo

Bread or Pizza dough
28 ounce canned or fresh tomatoes, chopped
Caciocavallo or provola (mild provolone)
1/2 cup pecorino or parmesan cheese grated
1/2 cup dry bread crumbs
4 anchovy fillets, chopped
1 medium onion, sliced and sautéed
Olive oil
Oregano or fresh Basil or Parsley, chopped
Salt and red pepper flakes to taste

Work some of the olive oil into the dough. Let rise for about an hour, cover with a cloth. Set in a warm place. In a frying pan with oil, gently fry the sliced onion, then add the parsley or basil and the tomatoes. Add salt and pepper and leave to simmer over low heat for 20 minutes or until reduced by half.

In an oiled, deep-sided baking pan. Spread the dough with your fingers and make a few dimples in the top. Add the sauce, sautéed onions, anchovies, and the cheese cut into pieces or grated. (caciocavallo or other cheese) pour over half the sauce and bake in a hot oven. After about 15 or 20 minutes, add more sauce and top with bread crumbs. Drizzle a little oil and replace in the oven for 30 minutes.

Sfincione is made or sold by Street vendors, especially in Palermo in the warmer months it is served at room temperature."Sfincione" does not refer to just any thick pizza. The genuine article is very simple: dough, with a simple sauce seasoned with salt, pepper, and onions. The cheese and anchovies are optional. Extra virgin olive oil should be used in the dough and topping.

Let's Eat!

Pizza Rustico

Rustic Pie

_Pizza Rustica or Pizza Chiena changes from north to south, east to west and every
region in Italy with thousands of recipes and none are the same._
_This recipe was a challenge. I consider my mother's pie was one of the best but
challenging. She has changed it through the years, so I do not have the exact recipe
nor ether did she. I have cut it down to a manageable size but if you want to make it
you will have to make adjustments to your taste, so saying that, I will give you a
guide as how to make it._

Pasta Frolla
(you may need to make extra to have enough for top and bottom-
depending the size of the pan)
4 cups flour
1/2 teaspoon salt
1 to 2 teaspoon baking powder
1/4-lb lard or unsalted butter
3 eggs, beaten
1/4 cup ice water or more if needed

Filling
3 pounds ricotta
5 to 6 eggs
1/2 cup grated Pecorino Romano
1/2-pound mozzarella, cubed
1-pound Basket cheese cubed (you can find this in Italian specialty stores
usually only at Easter)
1/2 pound Sopressata diced
1/2-pound prosciuttina (Peppered Ham) or 1/2 pound prosciutto, diced
1/2-pound sweet dried sausage, peeled and diced
1/2 cup chopped parsley
Egg Wash, 1 egg beaten with 1 tablespoon water
12-inch straight-sided cake pan well buttered

The Pasta Frolla

Combine dry ingredients in a bowl to mix. Cut lard or butter into flour and distribute evenly over dry ingredients in work bowl. Cut into flour (as you would for pie crust. Add eggs, water, and continue to need until dough forms a ball... If too dry add water as needed to form a ball like a pasta dough, if too wet add a little flour. Remove dough, press into a disk, wrap, and chill for at least two hours in the refrigerator.

The Filling

Place ricotta in a mixing bowl and stir in eggs one at a time; stir in remaining filling ingredients in order.

Preheat oven to 350 F and set a rack in the lower third. Divide the Pasta Frolla into 2 pieces. Roll 1 of the pieces thinly to line a 12-inch straight-sided roasting pan or possibly a large spring form pan. Pour in filling and smooth top. Roll the remaining dough. Cover and press at rim of pan to adhere and trim away excess dough even with top of pan. Crimp the edges to seal.

For egg wash, whisk egg and salt together. Paint dough with egg wash. Bake until the filling is set, and the dough is baked through, about 1 1/2 hours. Cool in the pan on a rack. (make it a least a day or two ahead it needs time to dry out a little) Serve from the roasting pan. To un-mold loosen the sides, place a platter on top and invert, removing pan. Replace pan with another platter and invert again, removing top platter. Serve cold or at room temperature. Refrigerate any leftovers.

This is a typical savory pie is served for Easter. Though many recipes for pizza rustica specify that the dried sausage, mozzarella, and other filling ingredients be layered, in the Neapolitan version, they are diced and added to the ricotta filling, making the resulting pie easier to cut.

Pizza Scarola

Escarole Pie

Crust
2 1/2 cups all-purpose flour
1 teaspoon salt
1/2 teaspoons freshly ground black pepper
1/3 cup extra-virgin olive oil, lard or unsalted butter
7 to 8 tablespoons ice water (if needed)
1 egg

Filling
3 pounds escarole
Coarse salt and crushed red pepper to taste (I prefer it spicy)
Extra-virgin olive oil
3 garlic cloves, peeled and finely chopped
3 to 4 anchovy fillets (or to taste) drained
1 /2 cup imported oil cured black olives, or Kalamata, pitted and sliced

In a large bowl, combine the flour, salt, and pepper. Drizzle with the oil, stirring with a wooden spoon until the mixture is crumbly (like a regular pie crust). Add egg and 2 tablespoons of the water and stir, adding more water as needed, until the mixture begins to hold together and form a smooth dough. Shape into a ball. Divide the dough and shape into two disks, one larger than the other. Wrap each disk separately in plastic wrap and let rest for 30 to 60 minutes.

Trim the escarole, Wash the leaves, and coarsely chop the escarole. In a pot combine the escarole with 1/2 cup water and salt. Cover and cook over medium heat until tender, about 15 minutes. Drain very well and let cool. Remove the excess water from the escarole by squeezing it firmly. In a skillet, heat the olive oil and garlic over medium heat. Add the escarole and stir well. Reduce the heat to low and cook, stirring occasionally for about 2 minutes. Stir in the anchovies and olives. Add salt and pepper to taste. Let cool.Preheat the oven to 375 F. Lightly oil a pie pan or an 8-inch round spring form cake pan.

On a lightly floured surface, roll out the larger piece of dough to a 15-inch circle. Fit the dough into the prepared pan, pressing it against the sides and letting the excess dough hang over the edge. Spoon the escarole mixture into the pan. Roll out the remaining dough to a 9-inch circle and place it over the filling. Roll up the edges of the dough together, pressing against the side of the pan to seal. Cut several slits in the top of the dough with a small knife to allow steam to escape. You can brush with a light egg wash before you bake.

Bake for 45 minutes or until lightly browned. Let cool. Serve at room temperature

My mother and both Grandmothers made these traditional recipes. There is nothing like this when you taste it. This is one of my favorites, I always try to make it on Christmas eve and Easter too. You can use pizza dough for this recipe. Serve at room temperature .

Pane di Pasqua

Easter Bread

1 envelope (2-1/2 teaspoons) dry yeast
1/2 cup warm water about 110 F
2 eggs, room temperature
2/3 cup sugar
8 tablespoons unsalted butter, or lard melted and cooled slightly
1/2 cup warm milk
2 teaspoon vanilla extract
1 tablespoon grated orange zest
1 teaspoon salt
5 to 5-1/2 cups flour

2 to 6 whole uncooked eggs, colored if desired
1 egg yolk beaten with 1 tablespoon water, for egg wash
Colored sprinkles (nonpareils)

The dough

Combine the yeast with the warm water in a bowl. Let stand until proofed, about 5 minutes. Stir to dissolve.

In a large bowl, beat the eggs. Beat in the sugar. Stir in the butter, milk, vanilla, and orange zest. Stir in the yeast mixture.

Add 5 cups of the flour and the salt. Stir until a soft dough forms.

Add enough of the remaining flour to make smooth dough.

Transfer the dough to a lightly floured surface and knead for a minute or two until very smooth. Shape the dough into a ball. Place in a buttered bowl.

Cover and let rise in a warm place until double in volume, about 1-1/2 hours.

Butter or use parchment paper on 2 baking sheets.

Punch down the dough and cut into 4 pieces. With your hands, roll one piece into a rope about 20 inches long. Repeat with another piece of dough. Lay the ropes side by side and loosely twist them together.

Place the ropes on the baking sheet. Bring the ends together to form a ring. Connect the ends. Place eggs around the wreath, tucking them between the ropes of the dough. Repeat with the remaining dough and eggs. Cover and let rise about 1 hour or until doubled in size. Preheat the oven to 350 F.

Brush the egg wash over the dough. Add the colored sprinkles (nonpareils) on top.

Bake the loaves for 30 to 40 minutes or until golden brown. Transfer the bread to wire racks to cool completely. Makes 2 Loaves

Throughout Italy, Easter bread making is a tradition. Breads vary from region to region some sweet some savory and many go by different names. Baking whole eggs into bread dough is part of the Easter tradition. Eggs are the symbol of fertility and new beginnings.

Garlic Knots

Pizza or bread dough
Olive oil
Kosher salt
Minced garlic
Grated Parmesan cheese
Chopped fresh parsley or Oregano

Mix olive oil, salt, garlic, cheese, parsley until the mixture is well combined. Transfer into a bowl. Cover and refrigerate until serving.

Preheat oven to 375 F.
Grease baking sheets or use parchment paper. Set aside.
On a floured surface, roll dough out about 1/2 inch thick. I used a pizza cutter to cut the dough in strips (about 8-10 inches) for the garlic knots. Brush the dough lightly with olive oil. Roll the strips in your hands to look like ropes and then tie in knots. Place the knots on a greased baking sheet and allow them to rise for another 10 minutes.
Bake at 400 degrees for about 15-20 minutes. Sprinkle the tops with salt. Cover with a clean towel and let rise in a warm place for 30 minutes. Bake until golden brown, 20-25 minutes.
When the knots come out of the oven, at once transfer them to a large bowl and gently toss with the garlic oil, Parmesan cheese, parsley, and extra coarse salt to taste. Serve warm.

I have never seen these in Italy, but I love them. Make them with any leftover bread, pizza, or focaccia dough.

Zeppole

2 cups flour
1 package dry yeast
1/2 tsp. salt
1 1/4 to 1 1/2 cups warm water (110 F)
Oil or Shortening for deep frying about 6 cups oil

Dissolve yeast in water. Add to mixed dry ingredients. Let rise for 1 hour. Dough should be wet and sticky
Heat oil to 350 F. Drop dough by teaspoon or tablespoons carefully into hot oil or shortening. Cook until browned on both sides and cooked through. Sprinkle with powdered sugar or toss with sugar and cinnamon and serve.

Zeppole with Anchovy

Dough for Zeppole
Anchovy fillets (about 1/2-inch piece per Zeppole)
Place an anchovy in the center and Fold dough over and make a ball.
Add to hot oil and cook until golden brown.
Serve hot or room temperature.

Calzone

Folded-over Pizza

Pizza dough (prepared pizza dough, raised)

Ricotta Prosciutto Stuffing
Ricotta
Mozzarella cheese cut in 1/4-inch dice
Prosciutto, cut in 1/4 inch diced
Romano cheese, grated
Fresh basil or Parsley, minced
Freshly ground pepper to taste

In a large bowl mix together ricotta, mozzarella, prosciutto, cheese, and basil. Salt and fresh ground pepper to taste
Shape dough into two small balls. Press each ball with palm of hand to make a disc. Roll dough with a rolling pin to 1/4 to 1/8-inch thickness and 8 to 10 inches round. Put filling on one half the disc, leaving a half inch border around the edges. Brush border with water, fold to make a half moon and seal together. Use fork or knife to puncture the top of calzone to allow steam to escape in cooking. Brush with egg wash if you like. Place on a lightly oiled or parchment lined baking sheet.
Bake on the middle rack of preheated 450 F ovens until calzone has a deep golden color, about 30 minutes. Serve at room temperature. Ricotta and prosciutto are classic, but you can use pieces of your favorite salami.
Calzone is a folded stuffed pizza that originated in Naples in the 18th century.

Pane Grattate
Breadcrumbs

2 to 3 cups Italian bread
1/4 cup grated Italian chees
1 to 2 tsp dried parsley
Oregano to taste
Salt and Freshly ground pepper
Dried garlic (garlic powder) to taste

Begin by drying your bread until it hardens. You can harden the bread in a low-temp oven. Break the bread in small pieces if you are using Italian bread in a processer.

After bread hardens grate or put it in the food processer, to make the crumbs. Add your remaining ingredients.

Store in the refrigerator (should be refrigerated because of the cheese)

This is only a suggestion and one of the very few times I use dry herbs. Flavor as you like.

Garlic Toasts

Italian loaf, cut into 1/2-inch-thick slices
2 tablespoons olive oil
I garlic clove, halved crosswise
finely chopped fresh flat-leaf parsley

Arrange bread slices in one layer on a baking sheet, then drizzle with oil and season with salt. Bake or broil, turning over once, until golden, about 10 minutes total. Transfer toasts to a rack to cool slightly, then rub lightly with cut sides of garlic and sprinkle with parsley.

Dolce

Dolce

Anise Biscotti

Cantuccini alle Mandorle

Biscotti Regina

Savoiardi

Struffoli/ Pignolata

Cenci

Pizzelle

Pignioli Cookies

Cuccidati

Pizza Dolce

Torta di Ricotta

Pastiera di Grano

Cuccia

Pan di Spagna

Cassata

Tiramisu

Cannoli Cream

Crema Chantilly

Crema Pasticcera

Macedonia Di Frutta

Arance Marinata

Fragole all Aceto

Pere al Vino

Zabaglione

Croccante di Mandorla

Pasta Frolla

Anise Biscotti
Italian Anise Toast

2 1/4 cup flour plus extra for kneading
1 cup granulated sugar
2 teaspoons baking powder
Pinch of salt
A large pinch anise seeds (optional)
3 large eggs, beaten if small use 4
1/2 cups butter melted
1 teaspoon anise extract or 1/4 tsp anise oil (A few drops vanilla or anisette liqueur, these flavorings are very strong it is all up to you and your taste)

Preheat oven to 350 F.
Butter and flour a baking sheet or use a non-stick liner.
In a large bowl, sift dry ingredients together. Make a well in the center of the mixture and add remaining ingredients. Mix thoroughly. Turn out on to a floured board. Knead lightly until the dough forms. Add more flour if necessary. Divide the dough in half. Shape dough into two cylinders about 1 inch high and 7 or 8 inches long. Place on prepared baking sheet leaving some room between them.
Bake 30 to 35 minutes until slightly browned on top. Remove from oven and let cool for 5 to 10 minutes.
Cut cylinders diagonally into 3/4-inch slices (with a serrated knife). Replace slices on baking sheet cut sides down. Bake for 15 minutes more, until nicely golden. Cool on wire racks. Anise Biscotti should be quite crisp. Cool and store in an airtight container.

Anise Biscotti are perfect for dunking in sweet wine or coffee.
Anise seed and anise essence should be the best quality for the most delicious results.

Cantuccini alle Mandorle
Almond Biscotti

5 to 6 eggs
1 cup granulated sugar
1 teaspoon vanilla or almond extract
1/4 cup (1 stick) unsalted butter, melted
4 cups flour
4 teaspoons baking powder
1/8 Teaspoons Salt
1/2 Teaspoons Cinnamon
1 to 2 cups chopped almonds

Place the almonds in a preheated 325 F oven and toast the almonds just until they begin to take on color. Cool, and coarsely chop.
Preheat oven to 375 F.
Mix eggs thoroughly. Add, cinnamon, salt. sugar, vanilla, and melted butter.
Add flour, baking powder and chopped almonds. Dough will be thick. Divide On a lightly floured surface, divide the dough in half, and form two loaves about 9 inches long and 2 1/2 inches wide and place on a lightly greased baking sheet.
Bake for 35 minutes, or until they are golden brown. Allow cooling for 5 minutes, then using a serrated knife then slice at a slight angle into 1/2 - 3/4-inch slices. Place these slices back on the baking sheet and cook an additional 5-10 minutes or until the cookies are golden in color and dry. Cool, and store in an airtight container.

These are called biscotti, but all cookies are biscotti in Italian. These are properly called Cantuccini. They are double-baked to get their crispness.

Biscotti Regina
Sesame Cookies

2 sticks unsalted butter at room temperature
1 cup sugar
3 eggs, lightly beaten
1 teaspoon vanilla (optional)
3 1/2 cups flour
1/4 tsp salt
2 1/2 tsp baking powder
Milk or light egg wash
1 cup sesame seeds or enough to coat all cookies
Flour for kneading dough
Greased cookie sheets (or Parchment paper)

Preheat oven 375 F
Mix the flour, salt, and baking powder in a bowl. Set aside.
Cream the butter and sugar together in a large bowl. (Electric mixer may do well)
Add the eggs and vanilla to the sugar-butter and mix well until fluffy.
Add the flour 1/2 cup at a time to the egg-butter mixture. Mix well after each addition.
Place the dough on a floured surface and knead until smooth.
Take small amounts of dough (about 1 Tablespoon or the size you prefer) and shape into little logs. Repeat with the remaining dough.
Dip each cookie log into the milk and then roll in sesame seeds until well coated.
Place on cookie sheet and bake at 375 F for 20 minutes or until browned. Remove from the tray and allow to cool. Store in are tight containers-they freeze well.

Sesame cookies with a cup of espresso in the afternoon and a glass of anisette on the side. The Best!

Savoiardi

Lady fingers

4 eggs, separated
2/3 cup sugar, divided
1 teaspoon vanilla extract
Pinch of salt
3/4 cup flour
Granulated sugar, optional

Separate the eggs. Beat the egg yolks with 1/3 cup of the sugar, salt, and the vanilla. Beat until very light colored about 5 minutes.

Beat egg whites until stiff, but not dry, and gradually beat in 1/3 cup sugar until whites are glossy and   stiff but not dry.

Fold egg yolk mixture gently into whites then fold in sifted dry ingredients.

Cover cookie sheets with parchment paper. Prepare a pastry bag with a tip (1/2-inch). Fill the pastry with half of the batter and pipe 3 1/2-inch fingers, 1 1/2-inches apart, in rows on the parchment paper. Sprinkle with granulated sugar (optional).

Bake at 375 F degrees for about 15 minutes until firm to the touch and golden. Remove the paper and fingers from the baking sheet and place on racks to cool. After cooling, remove fingers from the paper and use, or store between layers of wax paper in an airtight container. They freeze very well.

My grandmother would make these, and I remember how my grandfather would love to dunk them into his morning coffee. Try it !

Struffoli / Pignolata
Honey Balls

4 cups flour (1 lb.)
4-5 eggs
1/2 tsp. salt
Vegetabl Oil for Frying

Garnish
1 plus Cups Honey
1/4 cup sugar
Zest of 1 Lemon
Sprinkles (multicolored nonpareils)

In a large bowl, combine flour, egg, salt, and knead to form a firm dough, about 8 to10 minutes. (Just as if you are mixing Pasta) Cover with plastic wrap and refrigerate for1 hour or longer. To shape, pinch off small pieces and roll into logs about the width of your finger. Cut these logs into 1/4-inch pieces (They puff up, so you have to judge the size) and roll each into a ball shape. (I like them small maybe chick pea size) Continue shaping in this manner until you have used up all the dough.
Heat oil to 375 F degrees in a heavy pot and fry a little at a time until light golden brown. Drain on paper towels.

Once all your struffoli are cooked, heat the honey with the lemon zest in a saucepan or pot. Cook for 5 minutes to thicken the honey. Cool and then add to the cooked struffoli in a large bowl or pot and carefully stir until the struffoli are well coated (you can also pour the honey over the struffoli). Cool 5 minutes and then place on a large platter in the shape of a pyramid. Sprinkle with the candied sprinkles.
Crisp fried nut shaped puffs make an attractive centerpiece for a special occasion. A traditional Neapolitan holiday treat.

Cenci / Chiacchiere
Rags / Chatter

1 1/2 Cup All-Purpose Flour (more if needed)
3 Tablespoons Melted Butter
2 Tablespoons Granulated Sugar
1 Egg
2 Tablespoons Vin Santo, Wine or Rum
1/2 Teaspoon Vanilla Extract
Pinch of Salt
Oil for Deep Frying
Confectioners' Sugar

Place the flour and slowly add the other ingredients in a medium sized bowl mixing well. Form dough, and lightly knead for a minute or two. Cover with plastic wrap and let sit for an hour or overnight. Roll out onto a lightly floured surface until very, very thin (at least number 6 or thinner on a pasta machine). Use a fluted pasty wheel and cut pastry into strips or cut into thin strips about 6-8 inches long and 1 1/2-inch-wide, and gently tie into a knot. Fry in oil heated to 375 F. until golden. Drain on paper towels, and lightly dust with confectioner's sugar. This recipe can easily be doubled.

Fried pastries of this type can be found across Italy, particularly during the carnival season. The word Cenci means tatters or rags, which is what these pastries look like before you fry them.

The dough for Struffoli can be used to make Chiacchiere (chatter). Rolled out very thin cut and fried. Cover with the honey mixture and sprinkles or heavily covered with Confectioners' Sugar and for a special treat Sugar and cinnamon combo.

The Struffoli dough is the one I use most often to make Chiacchiere.

Pizzelle

Waffle Cookies

3 eggs
1 teaspoon vanilla or anise extract (start with one and increase to taste)
3/4 cup white sugar
1 3/4 cups all-purpose flour
1/2 cup butter, melted
2 teaspoons baking powder
Confectioners' sugar to dust

In a large bowl, beat eggs and sugar until thick. Stir in the melted butter and vanilla. Sift together the flour and baking powder, and blend into the batter until smooth. Let rest about 10 minutes.
Heat the pizzelle iron, and brush with oil. Drop about one or two tablespoon of batter onto each circle on the iron. You may need to experiment with the amount of batter and baking time depending on the iron. Bake for 20 to 45 seconds, or until steam is no longer coming out of the iron. Carefully remove cookies from the iron. Cool completely before storing in an airtight container.

Powdered sugar adds an elegant touch.

Pignoli Cookies
Pine Nut Cookies

2 pounds Almond Paste
1-pound confectioners' sugar
1 oz Honey
1/2 teaspoon lemon extract
1/2 to 1 teaspoon almond extract or to taste
4 egg whites
Pine nuts about 1 1/2 cups

Use a pastry chopper (or food processor) to break up the almond paste into a granulated form. Put in mixing bowl and gradually add the sugar, extracts and honey.

In another small bowl beat the egg whites slightly. Once the sugar is incorporated, add them into the sugar and almond paste mixture gently. Mix into paste form shape about the size of a walnut and flatten a bit (dough will be sticky) then add pignoli, press pine nuts into the top of the cookie (you want to cover the top with pine nuts). Bake on parchment paper on cookie sheet.

Bake 325 F for 15 to 20 minutes or until golden (do not overcook) Cool on wire rack. Store in an airtight container.

If you can get Mediterranean pine nuts, they are the best and worth the price.

Cuccidati

Sicilian Fig Cookies

Pastry

2 1/2 Cups All-purpose Flour
1/2 Cup Sugar
2 Teaspoons Baking Powder
1/4 Teaspoon Salt
6 Tablespoons Unsalted, Soft Butter
2 Large Eggs
1 Teaspoon Vanilla Extract

Dough

To make the dough, combine the flour, sugar, baking powder and salt in a large bowl. Cut the butter into the flour mixture until the mixture becomes pea sized pieces. Whisk together the eggs and vanilla and mix this into the flour mixture. Knead very briefly to create a smooth dough, adding a little ice water if the dough is too dry to work. Bring the dough into a ball, wrap in plastic wrap, and refrigerate for 1 hour.

Filling

2 Cups Moist Dried Figs (remove hard stems)
1/2 Cup Raisins (I prefer currents)
1 Cup Almonds or hazel nuts or both, Toasted and Chopped
1/3 Cup Honey
1/3 cup Rum (spiced Rum is nice)
1 Teaspoon Cinnamon
1/4 Teaspoon Nutmeg
1/4 Teaspoon fresh cracked black pepper
1/4 Teaspoon ground Clove
1 Tablespoon Orange Zest Finely Chopped

Frosting

Confectioner's Sugar and water to make a paste for icing and top with nonpareils.

To Complete

Place the figs, raisins in a food processor and pulse until finely chopped. Add the nuts and pulse briefly again. Transfer to a bowl and add the remaining filling ingredients. Stir well and set aside while you make the dough. (I let these ingredients sit for a couple of days at room temperature and even add more rum, like Fruitcake. Get it? If it soaks it up add some more, you get it)
Preheat the oven to 350 F.
Line baking sheets, with Parchment or silicon sheets. Cut the dough into 6 equal sized pieces, and place one on a lightly floured surface. Roll this dough to a thickness of pie crust about 1/4 inch roll a 9 X 5-inch rectangle. Trim the edges with a sharp knife and spoon a strip of filling down the center about 1 inch in width. Lightly wet the edges of the dough with water, and then close, by folding one edge over the filling, and then the other, pressing the edges to seal. Roll the log over on the seam and cut it into pieces 2 or 2 1/2 inches with a sharp knife. Place the cookies on a baking sheet about 1 inch apart. Continue using up the remaining dough in this manner. Bake for about 25 minutes, or until the cookies are lightly browned. Cool and lightly top with the icing powdered sugar and a little water and top with multicolored nonpareils. Store in airtight containers. Yield: depending on the size of the cookies.

Cuccidati are a traditional cookie very popular particularly in Sicily. You can use either light or dark figs but choose dried figs that are moist and tender. Walnuts can be substituted for the Almonds . I also like to add a little chopped chocolate to the filling which gives extra flavor to the cookie. To complete the cookie, you can either use colored sprinkles, or simply dust with confectioner's sugar before serving.

Pizza Dolce

*Sweet Pie (*Italian Cheesecake)

3 lbs. ricotta cheese
1 tbsp. orange peel (diced)
1 tbsp. lemon peel (diced)
1 tsp. Almond extract (optional)
1 tsp. Vanilla extract
6 eggs (grade A large) separated (beat the egg whites until form soft peaks)
1 1/4 cups sugar (I like it less sweet, so I use less sugar, 1 cup)
1/4 cup flour (for gluten free omit the flour) add 1 more egg

In a large bowl mix all ingredients ,except the egg whites. Beat with electric mixer until very smooth. Fold in beaten egg whites until just completely mixed (not over mixed)
Pour into a 9"- 10" (I use larger) spring form pan that has been buttered and dusted with sugar or flour.
Bake at 325 to 350 F, depending on oven for 50 to 60 minutes or until center is firm and top is lightly brown. Turn off oven let rest 10 to 20 minutes with door slightly open.
Best made a day or two before serving.
Insert knife around sides of pan to insure easy removal of spring pan sides.

Torta di Ricotta
Neapolitan Sweet Pie

The Crust
2 1/2 cups flour
2/3 cup unsalted butter
2/3 cup sugar
3 yolks or 1 egg lightly beaten

The Filling
1-pound fresh ricotta
2/3 cup sugar
1/2 teaspoon vanilla extract
1/2 teaspoon orange flower water (available at Italian specialty shops)
The grated zest of half an orange
2 egg yolks
Small amount of finely minced candied fruit if you choose (I do not use
it unless I can get the best quality)

Mix the flour and sugar and cream the butter. Combine the ingredients
of the dough, using a pastry cutter and working the dough as little as
possible with your hands. Form it into a ball and let it sit in a cool place
for an hour.

Put the ricotta in a bowl, combine it with the sugar, and beat the
mixture until it is smooth and creamy. Lightly beat the yolks and work
them into the mixture a bit at a time, and finally stir in the minced
candied fruit (if using it).

Divide the dough into two unequal pieces. Use the larger one to line a
buttered 8-inch pie or springform pan. Fill the pie with the filling.
Cover it with lattice strips cut from the second piece of crust, crimping
around the edges, and bake it in a moderate oven for about an hour. Let
it cool, and dust it with powdered sugar.

*Torte di ricotta, or ricotta pie, is an Italian cheesecake in a crust there are many
variations to Torte di Ricotta, some simple and others quite complex.*

Pastiera di Grano
Wheat Pie

Pasta Frolla (Flaky Sweet Pastry)
2 cups sifted flour
1/4 cup sugar
Pinch of salt
1/4 cup butter
3 egg yolks
1 tablespoon milk

Filling
3/4 lb.-soaked wheat, drained (this is the weight after soaking)
1/2 cup hot (scalded) milk
1 teaspoon salt
1 teaspoon sugar
1 1/2 lbs. Ricotta
1 1/2 cups sugar (I use a little less)
6 egg yolks, beaten
Dash of cinnamon (optional) 1/4 teaspoon
Grated rind of one lemon and one orange peel (I cut it into fine strips zest)
1/2 teaspoon Orange Flower Water (found in Italian specialty stores)
4 egg whites, beaten stiff
1 teaspoon vanilla

Wheat: The wheat should be rinsed with water and then placed in a large bowl. Add cold water to cover and let soak overnight in the refrigerator. Drain the wheat and place in a saucepan with enough cold water to cover. Cook over medium heat, stirring occasionally, for about 20 - 30 minutes until tender. Drain water, add 1/2 cup scalded milk, 1 teaspoon sugar, and boil for additional five minutes, until all liquid is absorbed. Remove from heat, let cool, while prepared wheat is cooling, prepare pasta frolla.

Pasta Frolla: Sift flour, salt, and sugar into a bowl, cut in butter with a pastry blender or with finger tips, to distribute the butter evenly through the flour. Stir in egg yolks one at a time, mixing with a wooden spoon. Work with hands until dough is manageable adding a little milk, if necessary, to hold together. Turn onto a lightly floured board and knead quickly until smooth. Form into a ball and chill and rest for at least 30 minutes or longer. Then divide ball into two parts, one larger than the other. Roll large piece on lightly floured board into a large disc, 1/8-inch thick, large enough to line a deep 10-inch pie plate. Butter the pie plate and line with pastry, leaving a 1/2-inch overhang. Roll out the smaller piece of dough 1/8 -inch thick and cut into 3/4-inch strips, for lattice work topping.

Filling: Beat ricotta and sugar together, adding 6 beaten egg yolks, vanilla, cinnamon, lemon rind, orange rind and Orange Water, blending well. Stir in prepared wheat and fold in egg whites. Turn into pie shell; arrange strips crisscross over filling, to edge; roll bottom overhang up over strips at edge and flute heavily. You can also brush crust and strips with a light egg wash.
 Bake in a preheated moderate 350 F. Oven for about 1 hour or until firm in center and crust nicely browned. Let cool completely. Dust with confectioners' sugar.
Makes 1 large or two 9 1/2 inch pies.

Note: Wheat berries are available in Italian specialty food store or health-food stores. You may find wheat that is presoaked and may not need the soaking.
There are many versions of this you will have to find your way (e.g. more wheat more flavoring less sugar etc.) also the moisture in the ricotta the size of the eggs so do not get discouraged it is traditional holiday pie and it is worth it.

Sometimes I was fortunate to be in my aunt Jenny's kitchen before Easter when she was baking. I would always watch how she would put a small piece of palm from Palm Sunday on her breads and pastries a symbol of Easter.

Cuccia

Wheat Berries with Ricotta

1 cup   wheat berries
Water
1/2 teaspoon salt
1 1/2 cups high-quality whole-milk ricotta
Sugar or Honey to taste
1/2 cup currants or raisins
Generous pinch cinnamon (optional)

Soak wheat in cold water to cover overnight in the refrigerator. Drain and place in a 3-quart saucepan along with the salt and enough water to cover by 2 to 3 inches. Cook at a slow simmer, partially covered, about 1 hour, or until tender. Kernels will open slightly.
Drain the wheat and combine it with the ricotta. Blend in honey to taste, and the raisins or currants. Turn into a deep serving bowl and dust with cinnamon. Serve warm or at room temperature in small bowls.
In southern Italy people eat wheat kernels with creamy ricotta, sweetened with sugar or honey and dried fruit to celebrate the feast of Santa Lucia on December 13.
You can cook the wheat a day ahead and keep it in the refrigerator.

Add some semi-sweet chocolate to taste or I like orange or lemon rind thinly sliced and a touch of cinnamon.

Pane di Spagna
Sponge Cake

Ingredients
5 large eggs, room temperature
1 1/2 cups sugar (I use a little less sugar)
1 1/2 cups flour
1 tsp vanilla
1/2 tsp grated lemon rind
Butter and flour for the pan

Separate the eggs putting the yolks in a large bowl and the whites in a smaller bowl. Add the sugar, vanilla, to the yolks and beat at least 5 minutes until a frothy consistency.

Beat the whites until they stand stiff.

Fold the whites into the yolk-sugar mixture. Turn it over slowly and gently until completely mixed.

Sift the flour (it is important).

Fold the flour slowly, a bit at a time, to the egg-sugar mixture.

Add the lemon peels, folding in gently.

Butter and flour a 9" x 13 cake pan or a spring form pan. Pour in the batter and bake at 350 F, for about 20 minutes. It is done when the cake is lightly browned on top or test with a toothpick.

Turn upside down to cool. Let cool before removing from pan.

Bake on a cookie sheet lined with parchment paper to create a sponge cake for rolled desserts (e.g. Jelly roll) with your choice of fillings. I love to use a cannolo filling spread on cake, roll dust with confectioners' sugar.

Cassata Siciliana
Cassata Cake

2 lbs. Ricotta
1/2 to 1 cup sugar or less
1 tsp. vanilla
2 1/2 dozen Savoiardi lady fingers (split in half) or Pan di Spagnia
sliced thin
1/4 cup Crème de Cocoa liquor or 1 tsp Rum extract
1/4 cup mini chocolate chips
1/4 cup candied fruit (optional) I prefer using fresh lemon rind
Split cherries (maraschino) and lady fingers for decoration

Combine Ricotta, sugar, vanilla, and liquor. Beat with electric mixer at medium speed about 10 minutes. When mixture is fluffy, stir in chocolate chips and candied fruit or lemon rind,
Line sides first and then bottom of 10-inch spring form pan with lady fingers pour in half of Ricotta mixture. Place another layer of split lady fingers down and pour rest of mixture in. Decorate top with 4 split lady fingers and cherries. Chill in refrigerator at least 8 hours or overnight. Unmold and serve.

A Sicilian sponge cake, layered and coated with sweetened ricotta, flavored with candied fruit, and chopped chocolate, and eaten as a celebration cake or dessert.
There are many versions of cassata cake some simple some very complicated. Experiment with the layers even using a pound cake. Make more layers or less; This recipe is my Mom's.

Tiramisu

Pick-Me-Up

8 medium eggs, separated
1 cup sugar
1-pound mascarpone
1 cup brewed espresso
1/3 cup sweet marsala, rum, or coffee flavored liquor
Savoiardi or ladyfingers
Cocoa powder for dusting

In a bowl, combine the egg yolks with the sugar. Using a hand mixer, blend on high speed for 3 minutes. Add the mascarpone, and beat for 2 minutes, or until the mixture is uniform and creamy. Set aside. In a clean bowl, beat the egg whites with a hand mixer until stiff peaks form. Gradually fold the beaten egg whites into the mascarpone mixture.

Assemble the tiramisu: In a bowl, combine the espresso and the rum. One by one, dip the ladyfingers in the coffee mixture, and arrange them in a single layer along the bottom of an 8- inch square baking dish. Spread a thin layer of mascarpone cream on top, followed by another layer of coffee- dipped ladyfingers. Continue until you have 3 layers of ladyfingers, and finish with a layer of mascarpone cream. Cover with plastic and refrigerate overnight. Sprinkle top with cocoa powder. To serve, slice into squares.

This is one of the original recipes with raw eggs. There are other ways to make it you can use a pastry cream and then mix with mascarpone and then add whipped cream. A good substitute is Pastry cream or Chantilly cream (PAGE 248 - 249)

Cannoli Cream

Ricotta cheese
Sugar or confectioners' sugar to the desired sweetness
A few mini chocolate chips (optional)
pure vanilla extract (optional)
fresh orange or lemon zest

Place the ricotta cheese into a fine mesh strainer and place it in the fridge to drain for at least 12 hours and up to 24 hours.
In a large bowl combine the drained ricotta cheese, add sugar to taste, some orange zest, vanilla extract, and mini chocolate chips (if using); mix well until smooth. Use at once or refrigerate until needed; filling can be made up to 24 hours in advance.
For a lighter cream to fill cakes and pastries add some whipped heavy cream. (not too much)

Crema Chantilly

Italians speak of Crema Chantilly they mean whipped cream folded into crema pasticcera (pastry cream)
Crema Chantilly, made by folding whipped cream into an equal volume of crema pasticcera; it combines the richness of creme pasticcera with a delightful lightness and is perfect for filling beignets or other pastries, or making layer cakes, or millefoglie. Try it and you will never go back to other creamy fillings.

This is Italian version; the French version is sweetened whipped cream with a hint of vanilla (crème diplomatique).

Crema Pasticcera

Pastry cream

6 tablespoons flour
2/1 to 3/4 cup sugar
1 to 1/2 vanilla bean or 1/2 teaspoon vanilla extract
4 to 6 egg yolks
2 cups whole milk
Pinch of salt.

In a medium saucepan, combine milk, 1/4 cup sugar, vanilla bean and seeds, and salt. Cook over medium heat until mixture comes to a simmer.

In a medium bowl, whisk together egg yolks, flour, and remaining 1/4 cup sugar. Whisking constantly, slowly pour about 1/2 cup of the hot-milk mixture into the egg-yolk mixture, 1/2 cup at a time, until it has been incorporated. Pour mixture back into saucepan, and cook over medium-high heat, whisking constantly, until it thickens, about 2 minutes. Remove and discard vanilla bean. Cool slightly and cover with plastic wrap, pressing it directly onto the surface of the pastry cream to prevent a skin from forming. Refrigerate until chilled, at least 2 hours or up to 2 days. Before using, beat on low speed until smooth (you can also whisk by hand).

Crema pasticcera, pastry cream, is one of the basic ingredients used in Italian pastries and cakes: it is the creamy custardy filling of the layer cake, or the cream you find in pastry, and the creamy base of your tarts. Italian desserts would not be quite the same without it.

Macedonia Di Frutta
Mixed Seasonal Fruit

Seasonal fruit, for example berries, peaches, cherries, grapes,
apricots, etc.
4 tablespoons sugar
The juice of one lemon
Banana, peeled and sliced fresh (optional)
Wash core and dice the fruit.
Sweet wine or liquor to taste.

Wash, core, and dice the fruit.
Transfer all the fruit in a bowl add the sugar, and the lemon juice,
wine or liquor. Combine very well together and place in the
refrigerator for about 1 hours Remove and let rest at room
temperature.
Serve in single serving bowls. Serve with fresh mint and a spoon of
mascarpone or whipped cream.

*Macedonia is a region of the Balkans, where many different populations live
together. Maybe this is the reason for the name of this dessert: all sorts of
different fruits in the same containers. There is no rule: any kind of fruit in
season can be used.*

Arance Marinata
Macerated Orange Slices

6 sweet juicy orange
4 to5 tablespoons sugar
1 lemon

With a sharp paring knife, cut peel, including all white pith, from 5 oranges; slice peeled oranges crosswise into 1/4-inch slices. Pick out and discard any seeds. Place slices in a large, shallow bowl; sprinkle sugar and zest of lemon over the top. Squeeze juice from remaining orange and half of the lemon over orange slices. Gently stir and toss orange slices. Chill in refrigerator, covered, at least 1 hour.
Just before serving, carefully turn slices over in juices two to three times. Serve chilled. with fresh mint.

These chilled orange slices are perfect as is, but if you want you can toss them with 2 tablespoons maraschino liqueur just before serving.

Fragole all'Aceto
Macerated Strawberries

1-pound fresh strawberries
2 tablespoons sugar
2 tablespoons (Good) balsamic vinegar
Fresh mint
Mascarpone or whipped cream (optional)

Clean and rinse strawberries cut them into slices. In a bowl, combine berries, sugar, and vinegar and stir well.

Pere al Vino

Pears in Wine

4 pears (preferably in season)
Red, white or Marsala wine
Whole cloves or cinnamon sticks
About 1/3 cup sugar or to taste
Whipped cream

Peel your pears (you can core and cut them into halves or quarters), as many as you want. Put them in a pot or saucepan, cover with red wine and cook until they are soft, add sugar, cloves, and cinnamon - as much as you want. Turn the pears so that all sides get equal treatment. By the time, the pears are finally soft, remove them and boil the wine mixture down to a thickened sauce. Let cool before eating. You can prepare ahead and refrigerate, bring to room temperature before serving. Serve with fresh whipped cream on the side (optional). Spoon sauce over the pears then serve.

You are now ready for a big treat.

Zabaglione

Wine Custard

8 egg yolks
1/2 cup sugar
1 cup Marsala wine

Bring a pot of water to a simmer over medium-low heat. Combine the egg yolks and sugar in a metal bowl and whisk until foamy. Set the bowl over the simmering water, without letting the bottom touch the water, and continue to whisk constantly. Gradually pour in the Marsala while continuing to beat, do not let it boil. Keep working-out that arm and whisk vigorously for a good 5 minutes, until the custard has doubled in volume and is very thick and yellow. Zabaglione is ready when it stands in soft peaks. Remove from the heat and serve or spoon into glasses and serve with fresh fruit, strawberries or plain torte or biscotti.

One of Italy's great gifts to the rest of the world, Zabaglione is a delicate but rich dessert or topping served in stemmed martini glasses with fruit.

Zabaglione can be folded into whipped cream to lighten it up like a Chantilly cream.

Croccante di Mandorla
Almond Brittle

4 Cups almonds
3 cups sugar
1/2 cup water

In a saucepan add sugar and cook on high heat. Continue to stir until sugar begins to sweat and liquefy add a bit of water to help if necessary, continue to cook until sugar turns into a deep rich brown color. Do not burn. Add almonds and mix well. Cook a few minutes making sure your almonds are fully coated. Remove from heat and quickly spread the hot almond/ sugar mixture on a cookie sheet to the desired thickness.
Let cool for at least 1 hour before breaking into pieces.

talian desserts Italians are well-known for mixing in different fruit, zests and peels in their cakes and pastries. They may even add some fruit liquor in their desserts, yet the taste will still be particularly light. Italians are not fans of adding to many sweeteners. Italian desserts show the flavors of the ingredients and not just simple sweetening thing up.

Pasta Frolla
Shortbread Pastry

2 1/3 cups flour
1/2 cup sugar (optional)
1/4 teaspoon salt
1/2 Teaspoon baking powder
3/4 cup unsalted butter, cold cut into cubes
1 egg and 1 yolk
Ice water if needed
The grated zest of a half a lemon (optional)

Mix the flour and sugar, salt, baking powder and butter. Combine the ingredients, handling them as little as possible to keep the butter from melting (a pastry blender makes this easier sometimes I use a food processor) add egg and mix until the dough comes together add water if needed to make a smoother dough, wrap in plastic wrap and let it rest for at least one hour or overnight.
When ready to use, roll out on a lightly floured work surface (do not overwork) and continue with your recipe.

Pasta frolla is quite similar to shortbread, and is used primarily to make pies, cookies and crostate. Also used in savory pies without the sugar and lemon rind.

Bevande

Drinks

Limoncello
Bicerin
Affogato
Espresso

Have lemons? Make Limoncello!

Limoncello transports you to Italy to all the charming sea towns on the Amalfi Coast. Known for narrow windy roads, beautiful citrus groves, and magnificent views of the Mediterranean Sea.

Always sipped icy cold after dinner.

Limoncello

Limoncello

8 to 10 organic lemons
1 (750 ml) bottles Everclear or other neutral high-proof alcohol
2 1/2 cups sugar
3 1/2 cups Filtered water

Wash and dry the lemons. With a vegetable peeler, remove only the yellow rind, leaving the pith intact. (Reserve juice from the lemons for another use.)

Place the lemon peels in a 4-quart or larger jar with a lid. (I have large wide opening glass jars with lids, but I first put plastic wrap on and then the lid) Add the grain alcohol, making sure the lemon peel is completely covered. Store in a cool, dark place, stir or shaking the jar once each day to agitate the lemon peel for 14 days.

After 14 days, bring the water to a boil in a large saucepan. Add the sugar and boil for 5 minutes remove from the heat, stirring until sugar is completely dissolved. Cover and let cool to room temperature.

Stir in sugar syrup to combine the liquids, about 1 minute (mixture will turn cloudy).

Remove the lemon peals, strain the contents of the jar. Discard the lemon peel.

Transfer back to the jar. Store for 1 week in a cool, dark place, stirring every couple of days.

After a week, transfer the Limoncello to smaller bottles that can be sealed with stoppers and stored in freezer. Store your Limoncello in the freezer to enjoy icy cold – it will not freeze. Serve directly from the freezer.

Note: Grain alcohol is also known as Everclear, after a company that labels it as such.

Not only is Limoncello delicious, it is easy and inexpensive to produce, having only a few simple ingredients and requiring just a bit of time to mature.

Bicerin

Creamy Piemontese Cocoa-Coffee

Hot Chocolate (very thick and creamy) made from milk and real
chocolate
Espresso coffee, sweetened to taste
Hot milk whipped to a creamy froth

A thick-sided glass, ideally stemmed, whose volume is about a cup.
Begin by filling the glass 1/4 filled with espresso. Follow the
espresso with hot chocolate, again a quarter, and finish with the hot
frothy milk (if you have an espresso machine, heat it with the steam
jet) also a quarter, making for a glass about 3/4 full. You will have a
thick dark layer surmounted by a creamy layer (do not stir), and you
should not be surprised if people request more.

*In Torino this is prepared from coffee, cocoa, and whipped milk. A little goes a
long way -- the word Bicerin, (Bee-chair-een) means little glass.*

Affogato
Drowned Coffee

Vanilla ice cream
Fresh brewed espresso (sweetened)
Put a scoop of vanilla ice cream into each cup
Pour espresso over ice-cream

Affogato in Italian means "drowned", and in this case it is cold
vanilla gelato being drowned by pouring freshly brewed espresso all
over it.
Add a splash of Amaretto or Frangelico and a biscotti or two on the
side are nice.

AFFOGATO!!
*The traditional Italian way—hot espresso turns the ice cream into an instant
float.*

Espresso

How to Make Espresso in a Moka Pot

Little stove-top moka pots can make good espresso, with minimal effort.

Fill the bottom reservoir of the pot, keeping the water below the pressure release valve. Place the funnel piece into the opening of the reservoir. Fill the top part of the funnel with ground coffee. Screw the top part of the pot onto the bottom.

Place the pot on the stove-top and turn up the heat.

In a few moments, the water and steam will force its way up through the coffee into the top part of the pot. Once the espresso stops flowing into the top portion, remove from heat. Pour and enjoy.

How to Make Coffee in a Plunger Pot

Plunger pots can make excellent coffee and are handy when you are away from home because all you need is hot water.

Heat your water to about boiling.

Remove the lid and plunger from your plunger pot. Add ground coffee into the bottom of the pot. The amount of coffee to use is up to you. About 1 heaping tsp per cup of water. Pour hot water over grounds.

Fit plunger into pot and press part way down.

Wait for a couple of minutes for the coffee to steep. Press the plunger completely down.

Pour and enjoy.

Lemon Peel or No?
I have never encountered lemon peel & coffee anywhere in Italy. I have seen it in New York also cinnamon-laced cappuccino. So, what, do Italians put in their espresso? Purists put nothing at all, and will tell you that caffe amaro, bitter coffee, is the only way to go.

All specialty coffees can be made from a standard espresso machine.

Espresso - *The base from which all specialty coffees are made - Hot water is forced through finely ground coffee to produce a maximum of 1 to 1.5 fluid ounces of beverage.*

Crema — *This is the golden head of the espresso, which is made of the oils extracted from the coffee during the brewing process.*

Doppio - *A double shot of espresso. (doppio is Italian for double)*

Espresso Con Panna - *A shot of espresso topped with whipped cream.*

Ristretto - *A restricted or short shot of espresso for an intense espresso taste.*

Macchiato - *Espresso with a small amount of steamed milk dappled on top to give a spotted effect.*

Cappuccino - *One shot of espresso, one-part steamed milk, one part foamed milk with an optional dusting of chocolate.*

Americano - *A standard sized cup of coffee made by dispensing a double espresso into hot water. Add milk to taste.*

Caffe Latte - *One shot of espresso mixed with steamed milk.*

Corretto - *Means 'corrected' or laced with an alcoholic spirit or liqueur.*

Caffè Decaffeinato Caffe Hag — *decaffeinated coffee*

Granita di caffe —*frozen, iced beverage (ice shavings of coffee) and topped with - con panna - optional whipped cream*

Many people helped me with this book, sharing their knowledge and experience or by offering their opinions on my endless inquiries.

My friend Barbara was enthusiastic about the book from the start and helped me over many hurdles, big and small. Her organizational abilities really helped me pull it together. My Uncle Al who I could always count on to provide his advice and friendship.

Let's Eat!

Index

(Antipasti)

Bread Salad 32
Bruschetta con Pomodoro 14
Bruschetta with Anchovies 16
Caponata 21
Capri Salad 19
Chickpea Fritters 30
Cipollini Agrodolce 23
Crostini with Chicken Livers 17
Fried Olives 27
Fried Zucchini Flowers 31
Frito Misto di Mare 33
Giardiniera -
Pickled Vegetables 25
Grilled Vegetables 20
Marinated Zucchini 24
Mozzarella in Carrozza 29
Mozzarella with Herbs 29
Parmesan Toast 14
Pickled Eggplant 26
Prosciutto wrapped
Asparagus 18
Sicilian-Style Olives 28
Stuffed Mushrooms 22
Tonno Sotto'Olio 15
Tuna Spread with Capers 18

Fresh Pasta

Cavatelli I II 40, 41
Crespelli 46

Gnocchi 39
Impasto di Spinaci-
Spinach Pasta 37
Manicotti 47
Pasta con Uova-
Basic Egg Pasta 36
Pici 38
Ravioli 44, 45
Tortellini 42
Trofie 38

Prima Piatti
Pasta

Bolognese Sauce 54
Burro e' Salvia 78
Cannelloni I II 74, 75
Crespelli Fiorentino 70, 71, 46
Fetttuccine con Fungi 61
Gnocchi alla Sorrentina 76
Lasagna al Forno 59
Linguini Fini with Anchovies 66
Orecchiette con Cime di Rapa 67
Paglia e Fieno 62
Pasta Aglio e Olio 64
Pasta all'Amatriciana 56
Pasta alla Carbonara 63
Pasta alla Norma 72, 73
Pasta alla Puttanesca 57
Pasta con Prosciutto e Piselli 65
Pasta Ricotta 77
Pasta Primavera 69
Penne Arrabbiata 55
Penne Rose 60
Pesto Sauce 79
Pomarola 52

Salsa di Besciamell 78
Salsa Marinara I II 50, 51
Spaghetti alla Gricia 58
Sugo di Carne Ragu 53
Trofe con Pesto 68

Polenta

Cooked Corn Meal 82
Fried Polenta 84
Polenta with Gorgonzola 84
Sausages and Polenta 83

Risotto

Asparagus Risotto 88
Rise e Bisi 89
Risotto Milanese 90
Risotto with
Porcini Mushrooms 91
Seafood Risotto 92

Zuppa

Battuto e Suffrito 111
Brodo di Manzo 98
Brodo di Pollo 97
Minestrone 104
Pasta e Ceci 108
Pasta e Fagioli 109
Pasta e Finocchi 101
Pasta Lenticchia 106
Ribollita 110
Scarola e Fagioli 102
Stracciatella 100
Tortellini in Brodo 99
Zuppa di Salsicce e Pasta 107

Secondi Piati

Bistecca alla Pizzaiola 119
Braciole-Cutina 139, 140
Cotoletta Alla Milanese 118
Melanzana Rollatini 133
Melanzana Ripieno come
Pannini 134
Ossibuchi alla Milanese 126
Parmigiana Di Melanzane al
Forno 132
Peperoni Ripieni al Forno 131
Petto d Pollo Impanato 138
Pollo Cacciatore 123
Pollo con Rosmarino 121
Pollo e Salsiccia 120
Pollo sotto Mattone 122
Polpette Semplici 129
Salsicce con Cime di Rape 136
Salsicce e Patate 136
Salsiccia con Peperoni 137
Saltimbocca Alla Romana 116
Scalopini alla Marsalla 114
Scalopini di Vitello Francese 117
Scalopini di Vitello Piccata 115
Spezzatino di Vitello con
Piselli 125
Stracotto di Manzo 124
Vitello Tonato 141
Zucchini Ripiene 130

Pesce

Baccalà 150, 151
Calamari Fritto 147
Fritto Misto di Mare 146

Gamberetti con
Aglio e Burro 153
Insalata di Frutti di Mare 152
Pesce alla Francese 148
Pesce alla Griglia 144
Pesce Spada alla Siciliana 145
Risotto a Frutta di Mare 160
Spaghetti allo Scoglio 157
Spaghetti con Vongole 158
Vongola Posillipo 155
Zuppa di Vongole e Cozze 156
Zuppa Di Pesce 154

Contorni/Verdure

Arrosto di Vedure 172
Asparagi Gratinati 171
X Broccoli Di Rapa con Peperoncino e
Aglio 164
Carciofi I II 166, 167
Cardi Fritti 185
Cavolo "Cappuccio" alla Siciliana 169
Cima di Rape con Patate 165
Fagioli all' Uccelletto 181
Fagiolino con Pomadoro 170
Frittella di Zucchinni 182
Fritto di Cardoni 182
Fritto Misto di Vedure 184
Giambotta 180
Parmigiana di Melanzane 179
Pastella Per le Frittura 183
Patata Dorato Fritte 178
Patata Schiacciata 177
Patate Arrosto 176
Peperoni I II III 174, 175 Piselli con
Prosciutto 171

Scarola in Padella 168
Spinaci Rifatti 168
Zucchini Fritti 173

Frittata
Frittata con Spinaci 190
Frittata con Zucchinni 189
Frittata di Asparagi 188
Frittata di Patate 191

Insalata
Insalata Verde /Green Salad 194
Fennel Salad 195
Fennel Salad with Oranges 196
Neapolitan Cauliflower
Salad 197
White Bean and Tuna Salad 198
Potato Salad and
Green Beans 199

Pane, Pizza, Focaccia

Biga 203
Breadcrumbs 227
Calzone 226
Ciabatta 206
Focaccia 213
Focaccia al Rosmarino 214
Garlic Knots 224
Garlic Toasts 227
Pane di Lardo 215
Pane di Pasqua 222
Pane Rustico 204
Pasta di Patate or Focaccia 212
Pasta per Pizza 208

Pizza di Cipolla 214
Pizza Fritta 211
Pizza Margherita 210
Pizza Rustica 218
Pizza Sauce 209
Pizza Scarola 220
Pizza Stromboli 216
Sfincione Di Palermo 217
Zeppole 225

Torta di Ricotta 241
Zabaglione 253

Bevande

Affogato 261
Bicerin 260
Caffe 263
Espresso 262
Limoncello 259

Dolce

Anise Biscotti 230
Arance Marinata 251
Biscotti Regina 232
Cannoli Cream 248
Cantuccini alle Mandorle 231
Cassata 246
Cenci /Chiacchiere 235
Crema Chantilly 248
Crema Pasticcera 249
Croccante di Mandorla 254
Cuccia 244
Cuccidati 238
Fragole all Aceto 251
Macedonia Di Frutta 250
Pan di Spagna 245
Pasta Frolla 255
Pastiera di Grano 242
Pere al Vino 252
Pignioli Cookies 237
Pizza Dolce 240
Pizzelle 236
Savoiardi 233
Struffoli/ Pignolata 234 Tiramisu 247

CPSIA information can be obtained
at www.ICGtesting.com
Printed in the USA
FSHW021819031119
63704FS